TENNIS SHORTS

TENNIS SHORTS

1,001 OF THE GAME'S FUNNIEST ONE-LINERS

GLENN LIEBMAN

CB
CONTEMPORARY BOOKS

Library of Congress Cataloging-in-Publication Data

Liebman, Glenn.
    Tennis shorts : 1,001 of the game's funniest one-liners / Glenn
Liebman.
        p.   cm.
    Includes index.
    ISBN 0-8092-3075-5
    1. Tennis—Quotations, maxims, etc.   2. Tennis—Humor.
I. Title.
GV996.L49   1997
796.342′02′07—dc21   97-7162
                                                                              CIP

To my editor, Nancy Crossman, and my agent, Philip Spitzer—thank you for your steadfast belief in the concept and marketability of sports humor. It is an honor working with such classy and talented professionals.

ACKNOWLEDGMENTS

First, thanks must go to the people who made this book possible—the great wits of tennis: Bud Collins, Martina Navratilova, Billie Jean King, Jimmy Connors, Ilie Nastase, John McEnroe, and so many more.

As always, there is a laundry list of people to thank for their help and encouragement over the years. But I've learned that despite my best efforts to acknowledge everyone, I always end up offending those whom I have inadvertently left out. That's why I'm using the KISS (Keep It Simple, Stupid) method of thanking people this time.

In addition to being the author of the Shorts series, I am the New York state director of the Alliance for the Mentally Ill. One of the best perks of my job is working with some wonderful advocates for families with children who have mental illnesses. There are few better advocates and few better tennis players than my good friend Steve

Greenfield. He is one of the world's most decent, intelligent, and honorable people.

Another great advocate is my buddy Harvey Rosenthal. No one works harder or is more dedicated than he is; plus, he does it all with a tremendous sense of humor. If life were like tennis, Steve and Harvey would be the world's best doubles team.

Thanks to my dad, Bernie, and my late mom, Frieda, who taught me the importance of a loving home and good friends. And thanks to Bennett, easily the best brother in the world, to whom I will be forever grateful for taking me to my first U.S. Open when I was a little squirt.

Speaking of little squirts, I'd like to thank my son, Frankie Jay. Besides being a genius (he does the best Edward G. Robinson imitation of any two-year-old) and a superstar athlete, he is the greatest kid I've ever known. I'm lucky to have him.

I'm even luckier to have my wife, Kathy. Over the months I worked on this book, she never complained about my working late; despite the disruptions to her life, she did everything possible to help me finish the manuscript. She continues to be my source of strength and my best friend.

INTRODUCTION

When I think about tennis, I think of the U.S. Open—but not Flushing Meadows, the current home of the Open. My memories are of the beauty and splendor of Forest Hills. When I was growing up in Long Island, the site of the Open was just a long stone's throw from my house. (However, the stone would have to have been thrown by Roberto Clemente.) Throughout my teenage years, my buddies and I were regulars at the tournament.

If you chose not to attend a match at the main court at Forest Hills, you could visit the outside courts and be one of a dozen or so people watching a match featuring a young Jimmy Connors or perhaps an aging Pancho Gonzales. I remember an afternoon when I was the only spectator watching Rosie Casals and Billie Jean King on a practice court. Then there was the time I sat next to a guy named Nastase who jokingly harassed a linesman during an obscure match about a mile from center court.

Perhaps no other sport has such clearly defined "good guys" and "bad guys" as tennis does. You can easily envision them wearing white hats or black hats as they compete against each other: white hats—Arthur Ashe, Rod Laver, Billie Jean King, Pete Sampras, Chris Evert; black hats—Jimmy Connors, Ilie Nastase, Andre Agassi, John McEnroe (of course).

As much as I disliked the players in black hats, however, I've learned that time heals all sports wounds. My antipathy to Connors gradually turned to respect as he made a series of amazing comebacks at the U.S. Open. In the case of McEnroe, my son and I saw him a few months ago at a World Team Tennis match in Schenectady, New York. No one cheered harder for him than I did. His obvious love of the game and his tennis brilliance have outweighed the negatives of his past.

The pragmatic reason for my newfound respect for Connors and McEnroe is that they are very funny men and are quoted throughout this book. I owe them and many others, such as Martina Navratilova, Bud Collins, and Ilie Nastase, a debt of gratitude for making this book possible.

Sit back, take a strawberries-and-cream break, and enjoy tennis's funniest lines.

"I don't want to see the future. The present is hard enough."

> *Boris Becker, asked about his future*
> *after winning Wimbledon at age 17*

"When I was 40, my doctor advised me that a man in his 40s shouldn't play tennis. I heeded his advice carefully and could hardly wait till I reached 50 to start again."

> *Hugo Black, former Supreme Court*
> *justice*

"Now that I'm 20, it's downhill all the way, I suppose."

> *Bjorn Borg*

"Steffi's so nice. And she's not an old person. She wears an MTV shirt."

> *Jennifer Capriati, at age 14, on the*
> *21-year-old Steffi Graf*

"It was the greatest feeling of my life. I mean, here I was playing a legend, a ledge."

> *Jennifer Capriati, at age 14, on playing Martina Navratilova*

"Reincarnation."

> *Rosie Casals, aging veteran, asked how she made it to the fourth round of the U.S. Open*

"Heidi and Lolita do the U.S. Open."

> *Bud Collins, during the 1996 U.S. Open, where 15-year-old Anna Kournikova and 15-year-old Martina Hingis both played in the quarterfinals*

"This isn't like going to see an old-timers' game in baseball where you say, 'It's nice to see they're still alive.' These guys are much more than alive."

> *Bud Collins, on the Grand Masters, an event for players 45 and over*

"My current's a little low."

> *Jimmy Connors, asked if he still had the same electricity he had as a young kid*

"The problem is that when you get it, you're too damned old to do anything about it."

Jimmy Connors, on experience

"I have no complaints. If I hadn't made it to 33, I'd have a complaint."

Jimmy Connors, on turning 33

"I'd like to make it to 1990."

Jimmy Connors, in 1989, on his goal for 1990

"Underdog, overdog, I'm just an old dog."

Jimmy Connors, at age 34, asked how he felt about being an underdog in competition

"It is time for somebody to take my place. But if they don't want it, I'm not going to give it to them."

Jimmy Connors, on doing well at the U.S. Open at age 39

"The first 20 years I was learning to play tennis. The second 20, I've been playing. I'm a young man when it comes to playing."

Jimmy Connors, at age 40

"Less hair, more wrinkles, same forehand, same serve."

Jim Courier, comparing his form to that of a year before

"Yeah, it makes me feel younger."

Chris Evert, at age 25, asked if she still wanted to be called Chrissie

"They'll show up in wheelchairs."

Peter Fleming, on he and McEnroe facing 37-year-old John Newcombe and 43-year-old Fred Stolle in the '81 U.S. Open doubles semifinals

"I don't think of this as a sunset. I think of it as a sunrise."

Andres Gomez, on winning the 1990 French Open at age 30

"They have more fun. They were born before Walkmen, so you can talk to them and stuff."

Tom Gullikson, on joining the over-35 Grand Champions tour

"I don't say she's too old to play, do I?"

Martina Hingis, on Martina Navratilova saying that Hingis was too young to turn pro at age 14

"Will you please name me a better hitter than Ted Williams, a better singer than Enrico Caruso?"

Jack Kramer, supporting his claim that players from the 1930s could beat players from the 1970s

"We played once before in juniors. I was in the under-18s and he was in the under-2s."

Johan Kriek, asked if he had ever played 17-year-old Michael Chang

"I'll go out and get a regular job when nobody is willing to pay me to do this one, when nobody puts up the money, and no fans show up and watch me play. That's when."

Bob Lutz, explaining his decision to play in a 35-and-older league

"This is increasingly a very young man's game. But come on, mate, 30 isn't old. I'm not a dinosaur."

Wally Masur, on making it to the semifinals of the U.S. Open at age 30

"It's not a matter of age. It's a matter of tennis."

Andrei Medvedev, on his success at age 18

"The eyes, not the legs, are when you lose that fraction of a second."

Gardnar Mulloy, on getting older

"I've been in the twilight of my career longer than most people have had careers."

Martina Navratilova

"I figured if he could do it at 39, I could do it at 34. I'm a spring chicken next to him."

Martina Navratilova, comparing her success in the '91 U.S. Open to that of Connors

"Inspire a few people to get off their fat butts and lose some weight."

> *Martina Navratilova, asked what*
> *message her and Connors's success in*
> *the '91 U.S. Open should send to*
> *people*

"Should Van Gogh have stoped painting at an early age?"

> *Martina Navratilova, on attempting*
> *to win her tenth Wimbledon at*
> *age 35*

"He's calling his parents after he wins. I'm calling my children."

> *John Newcombe, on 17-year-old*
> *Bjorn Borg*

"When we played, the Dead Sea wasn't even sick."

> *Fred Perry, at age 80, on himself*
> *and 83-year-old Ellsworth Vines*

"Most of today's men are a bunch of bums. Their shirttails hang out, their navels are on show, and, of course, they need to shave."

> *Ted Schroeder, 1949 Wimbledon*
> *winner, on players of the '90s*

"A sport so starved for luminence that it continually plucks babies from their incubators and forces them to shine despite the effects of the most damaging ultraviolet rays."

Cindy Shmerler, tennis writer

"Older champs get nervous playing young twerps."

Pam Shriver, on reaching the U.S. Open finals at age 16

"This is the first time I've fulfilled the fantasy of a middle-aged man."

Pam Shriver, on beating a middle-aged man at a "Play a Pro" contest in Texas

"I don't know where they're coming from, but I wish they'd send them back."

Wendy Turnbull, on losing to young and talented new players

"Looks like he missed the last train to Woodstock with neon-colored spandex. . . . He's tennis's flower child gone to seed."

Mr. Blackwell

"He's as understated as Caesar's Palace."

Tom Callahan, columnist

"Undoubtedly Nancy Reagan's astrologer and Hillary Clinton's psychic would advise Agassi to steer clear of Tennessee."

Bud Collins, after Agassi lost in the first round of the '96 French Open to Chris Woodruff and the first round of the '96 Wimbledon to Doug Flach, both graduates of the University of Tennessee

"His mind is pretty much blank these days. He's in love and he has enough money to pay off the national debt."

Bud Collins, explaining Agassi's 1996 slump

"I enjoy playing guys who could be my children. Maybe he's one of them. I spent a lot of time in Vegas."

Jimmy Connors

"There are a lot of little kids who run off at the mouth, and sometimes it comes out of their. . . ."

Jimmy Connors, on the early petulance of Agassi

"He'll give most of what he's got for a while. Then he'll stop. Then he'll get fat and something will happen and he'll come back again. That's just him. He's unique."

Jim Courier

"Which attitude is this? Is this the new attitude or is this the new, new attitude?"

Jim Courier, after Agassi claimed to have adopted a new attitude

"When he sees the other guy going for his towel, that's when Andre can really put the hammer on the guy."

Brad Gilbert

"I don't like tennis and I don't like golf; they're not contact sports. But I like that Andre Agassi. He can play defensive back for me anytime."

Jerry Glanville

"It's difficult, because Agassi is like Jesus wherever he goes."

Yevgeny Kafelnikov, after beating Agassi in the first round of a Monte Carlo tournament

"In my eyes there aren't too many similarities between Andre and Bambi."

Todd Martin, asked after beating Agassi in the fourth round of the '94 Wimbledon if he felt like the man who shot Bambi

"It's easier to be a jerk."

John McEnroe, on Agassi's rude on-court behavior

"He hits the ball harder than anyone I've ever played."

John McEnroe

"The only thing I like about his life is he's got a private plane."

> *Pete Sampras, comparing his lifestyle*
> *to that of Agassi*

"He plays like a Zen master."

> *Barbra Streisand*

"He's very evolved, more than in his linear years. He's very in the moment."

> *Barbra Streisand*

"My explosive scoring guy would be Agassi. He's spectacular, he can make the big play, the dipsy-do-dunkaroo."

> *Dick Vitale, on his all-tennis team*

AGENTS

"Behind every great man usually stands a press agent."

> *Bud Collins*

"In college basketball, there are all sorts of rules that are always bent, frequently broken. In tennis, there are no rules."

John Feinstein, on agents who recruit young tennis players

"Live artists can be tough to deal with. They look at dealers like tennis players look at agents: not as equals but as necessary evils."

John McEnroe, on expanding his art gallery

ARTHUR ASHE

"I would like to go out on the court for one match and be a complete jerk. It would be extremely out of character for me, but it would be interesting to experience what it's like."

Arthur Ashe

"He was an ambassador of what was right. He was an ambassador of dignity. He was an ambassador of class."

Bryant Gumbel

"Arthur Ashe was in the tradition of great leaders. He earned that status not by proclaiming it, but by living it."

Jesse Jackson

"At the tensest moment, he goes for all but the impossible. He is predictably unpredictable. He is unreadable."

John McPhee, writer, on the beauty of Ashe's game

"It would be akin to offering Ted Williams your thoughts on hitting a baseball."

Al Michaels, asked if he added his own commentary when announcing tennis matches with Ashe

"Everything he's done, he's done well. I don't know how you do it any better."

Tony Trabert

TRACY AUSTIN

"When Tracy was eight, she would beat the best ladies at the local tennis club and then go over to the baby-sitting area and play in the sandbox."
Jeanne Austin, Tracy's mother

AUSTRALIAN OPEN

"You're playing in, like, your first tournament of the year, and already it's a Grand Slam."
John McEnroe, on how difficult it is to get up for the Australian Open

"The facilities are so poor that you just can't pretend this is a major event."
John McEnroe

"But that won't give me a free hand to hold the beer."

> *Billy Carter, brother of former*
> *president Jimmy Carter, while being*
> *taught Chris Evert's two-handed*
> *backhand*

"The backhand is like a bad date—you don't want to go through with it, but, since you have to, the sooner it's over the better."

> *Bill Cosby*

"The only good backhand I ever ran into was my mother's. She used it across my mouth."

> *Alan King*

"I have a $40,000 forehand and an 11-cent backhand."

> *Alan King*

"If my child ever acted like them, that would be the last time he'd play tennis."

> *Jim Courier, on the behavior of*
> *Jimmy Connors and Ilie Nastase*

"Tennis doesn't need brashness or bad manners. The sport's bigger than any individual."

> *Roy Emerson*

"I hope people remember me for what I accomplished in the sport, that I've given something to the game. I don't want to go down as Ilie Nastase Jr."

> *John McEnroe, on his bad-boy image*

"Let all us bad boys go away and then what happens? The game was so boring before we came along."

> *Ilie Nastase, on himself, McEnroe,*
> *and Connors*

"What I did in the '60s would be G-rated today."

> *Dennis Ralston, 1960s bad boy, on*
> *the behavior of '70s and '80s players*

BALL BOYS

"I don't care, throw it anyway."
>*Art Larsen, after he asked a ball boy*
>*for a ball and the boy said he didn't*
>*have any left*

BATTLES OF THE SEXES

"We won't accept Bobby in our tournaments. Not even in drag. The only way we'll let him enter is if he gets the operation and the silicone treatments."
>*Judge Bookman, on Bobby Riggs*
>*asking to join the women's tour after*
>*defeating Margaret Court*

"I've always said Bobby Riggs did more for women's tennis than anybody."
>*Rosie Casals, on Riggs losing to*
>*Billie Jean King*

"He's an old man, he walks like a duck, he can't see, he can't hear, and besides, he's an idiot."
>*Rosie Casals, on Riggs*

"Two sets of rubbish that last only half an hour."

Pat Cash, asked his opinion of women's tennis

"If there was a top women's game on and I went out and practiced with Becker, people would watch our practice game."

Pat Cash

"Sometimes a shorter opera is much better than a long one."

Bud Collins, responding to claims that women shouldn't get as much money as men because they play best of three instead of best of five

"Out fishing."

Margaret Court, asked what she was doing on the day of the Riggs–King match

"It meant something because she won."

Frank Deford, on the significance of Billie Jean King defeating Bobby Riggs in the Battle of the Sexes

"My brother still beats me, and he's not even ranked. Martina would lose to the 1,000th man."

Chris Evert, on Guillermo Vilas's claim that Martina Navratilova would lose to the 1,000th-best male player, which Navratilova disputed

"The level of play is a zillion years below the men's."

Vitas Gerulaitis, on women's tennis

"Billie Jean went from Riggs to riches."

Bob Hope, on the money King reaped after beating Riggs

"We women did enough for Bobby Riggs. He became a big man long after his day."

Billie Jean King, on a possible rematch with Riggs

"The drop shot and volley heard 'round the world."

London Times, *on the King–Riggs match*

"I wouldn't play a girl for a million dollars. Even if I played horribly, I'd beat Martina."

John McEnroe

"Nobody knows me when I was the best player in the world in 1939, when I won Wimbledon. Now I'm over the hill, but I'm a star."

Bobby Riggs

"I'll tell you why I'll win. She's a woman, and they just don't have the emotional stability."

Bobby Riggs, on Billie Jean King

"She was bewitched, bothered, bewildered, and mesmerized into the worst match played by a good player ever."

Bobby Riggs, after easily defeating Margaret Court before facing Billie Jean King

"Women are brought up from the time they're six years old to read books, eat candy, and go to dancing class. They can't compete against men."

Gene Scott, predicting that Bobby Riggs would easily defeat Billie Jean King

"Bobby's going to beat the kid. . . . He's got all the shots."

> Pancho Segura

"I think it's silly for him to pick on girls, because he's having his own trouble with the guys at the moment."

> Pam Shriver, on Vitas Gerulaitis's put-downs of women's tennis

"On campuses people were hanging out of their dorm windows celebrating. The match had enormous symbolic importance."

> Gloria Steinem, on the impact of the Battle of the Sexes

"I haven't watched women's tennis in twenty years, and I have no interest to watch for the next twenty."

> Ion Tiriac, asked who he thought would win the 1986 U.S. Open women's final

BEAM ME UP

"He'd be much less likely to make unforced errors."

> *William Shatner, on how Mr. Spock would compare with Captain Kirk in tennis*

"If Kirk was a tennis player, he'd just take out his stun gun and blaze ahead."

> *William Shatner, on Captain Kirk as a tennis player*

BORIS BECKER

"I'd be looking straight ahead and the ball would already be past me. Next time I'll wear a cap and chest protector."

> *Paul Chamberlain, on playing Becker*

"The only way to break Becker on grass is if he hits two double faults, you hit a lucky return, and at love–40 he falls down accidentally before he hits the volley."

Mikael Pernfors

"Like all artists, he has to bring something extreme to his work. . . . He will always live on his emotions."

Ion Tiriac

BEVERAGE OF CHOICE

"Well, yes, naturally. Fred and I usually have a beer at five o'clock."

John Newcombe, asked if playing doubles with Fred Stolle at the unusual time of five P.M. would interfere with his schedule

"Hard to say. He probably didn't start till he was 10."

John Newcombe, asked if 16-year-old Pat Cash would keep up the tradition of Australian beer drinkers

"Beer will be enough for me. Where I come from, that's considered champagne."

> *Tony Roche, on being asked to*
> *celebrate a World Team Tennis*
> *championship with champagne*

"The great thing about playing tennis is that you forget your troubles for two hours and when you're finished, everything you do is better. Even the beer tastes better."

> *Bill Talbert*

BILLIE JEAN

"Billie Jean was Joan of Arc in a miniskirt."

> *Bud Collins, on King's impact*
> *on tennis*

"No man or woman in tennis has made such an extraordinary triple thrust as Billie Jean in advancing herself, women, and the game as a whole."

> *Bud Collins*

"I'm not a total believer in female equality—but when I play with Billie, that's different. I'm a believer. I'm happy to share my check with her."

Owen Davidson, on being her mixed-doubles partner

"Billie was the leader of the rebellion, and Chris the next president who provided stability."

Jerry Diamond, on the revolution in women's tennis

"She put money in my pocket and the pockets of all women tennis players."

Chris Evert

"On the court she's an evil, merciless bastard. Totally ruthless. She'll do everything and anything within the rules to win."

Frank Hammond, referee

"No one changes the world who isn't obsessed."

Billie Jean King

"I think the women should give Billie Jean five and a half percent of every paycheck they get."

John McEnroe

BJORN AGAIN

"If Borg's parents hadn't liked his name, he might never have been Bjorn."
Marty Indike

"It was like watching someone take off his underwear in public."
Gene Scott, on the unsuccessful comeback of Bjorn Borg

BODY PARTS

"He goes after his opponents like one of the tentacular Hollywood creatures attacking a deep-sea diver."
Bud Collins, on the 6'5" Andres Gomez and his long arms

"They wanted an arm and a leg."
Martina Navratilova, on why she decided not to insure her left arm through Lloyd's of London

"If I like it, I might have a job done on it."
> *Martina Navratilova, requesting that
> the nose on her wax likeness at
> Madame Tussaud's Wax Museum be
> shorter than her own*

BRITISH TABLOIDS

"Comic books for adults."
> *Rex Bellamy, tennis columnist for the*
> London Times

"What the chopping block at the Tower of London was to Anne Boleyn, the Wimbledon interview room is to the tennis players."
> *Thomas Bonk, sportswriter*

"Here in England all you write about is people's private lives. You're trash. All you write is trash."
> *John McEnroe*

"I don't mind a lie here and there, but it should at least be realistic."
> *Martina Navratilova*

"The trouble is they create such a furor that American papers react to the reaction."

Martina Navratilova, on the tabloids

"Playing Wimbledon is like being abducted by a UFO—you are snatched up into a beam of blinding light, intimately probed and examined by strange beings, and then returned to earth dazed and frightened."

Scott Ostler, syndicated sportswriter

BRUSH UP YOUR SHAKESPEARE

"Coriolanus is John McEnroe. Coriolanus was a great athlete who fought battles in public but hated the crowd that came to watch him, and who felt superior to people who provided him with stardom. I can believe in Coriolanus because McEnroe exists."

Ian McKellen, British actor, on his role in Shakespeare's Coriolanus

DON BUDGE

"I was to keep up the pressure at all times, never let up, so that playing me would be a generally unnerving and unpleasant experience."
Don Budge

"It was like playing against a brick wall."
Sidney Wood, tennis star of the 1920s, on Budge

MARIA BUENO

"She was such a beautiful player. I used to watch her play, and not watch the ball at all."
Françoise Durr

"Not only is she the most graceful of all players—but she uses every shot known to the game and all of the court."
Al Laney, tennis writer

CALIFORNIA,
HERE I COME

"I don't like it. I go to a restaurant and everyone is 100 or 150 years old."

> *Goran Ivanisevic, on playing in Palm Springs, California*

"I don't hate this place. I am a year older. Now I am closer to their age."

> *Goran Ivanisevic, discussing Palm Springs a year later*

MARY CARILLO

"She is employed simply to help sell more Perrier."

> *John McEnroe, on why Carillo is announcing the men's matches on the pro tour*

CHAMP

"Being a champion is all well and good, but you can't eat a crown."
Althea Gibson

"Whenever I hear anyone call me champ, I think there's something behind it."
Althea Gibson

MICHAEL CHANG

"He of the deep pockets and short arms."
Andre Agassi, good-natured comment about Chang's spending habits

"It isn't over until the fast laddie sinks."
Bud Collins, on Chang's ability to track down every shot

"Small wall of China."
Bud Collins

"Chang is like a fly, a little mosquito. Everywhere he is just running and running and you have to win points three times to win one point."

Goran Ivanisevic

"The role of terrier to a mailman."

John Jeansonne, Newsday *columnist*

"The crown prince of patience."

Curry Kirkpatrick, Sports Illustrated *columnist*

"He's like a fighter who fights you three minutes of every round, a ballplayer who has a good at bat every time."

Jim Murray

"Like hitting against a barn door, the ball always comes back."

Pete Sampras

"The point is never over with him—not until the ball bounces twice."

Pete Sampras

CHEATS

"I prefer to cheat."
William Shatner, on his tennis game

CHOKE HOLD

"I don't care who you are, you're going to choke in certain matchups. You get to a point where your legs don't move and you can't take a breath."
Arthur Ashe

"Basically, the reason you choke is that you don't have the strokes."
Vic Braden

"I told them I would prepare for the match. I'd go to St. Patrick's."

> *Sherry Acker, on telling friends how she was getting ready for her match in the U.S. Open against Chris Evert*

"Chris Evert goes to the net every other April, but she goes to the bank every Monday."

> *Vic Braden*

"What in the world can be boring about hitting a perfect ball?"

> *Mary Carillo, on people who call Evert's game boring*

"Chris is so great because when she misses she looks around as if something is wrong."

> *Natasha Chmyreva*

"If the Taj Mahal vanished from their midst, the good folks of Agra would no doubt carry on. But they'd have a terrible feeling that something wonderful was missing."

> *Bud Collins, on Chrissie's retirement*

"She's got the same game as me, but much better. I have the feeling that I have my head against a wall all the time, without getting anyplace."

Françoise Durr

"We make quite a team. Between us, we've won 18 Grand Slam singles titles."

Dick Enberg, on working with Evert on television

"We can't be comfortable with a schoolgirl who's so unemotional, so professional."

Ann Haydon Jones, during the early part of Evert's career

"Chris always looks like she's going to win. All the great players are like that even if they're more emotional or experienced than she."

Billie Jean King

"Break up Chris Evert."

Curry Kirkpatrick, on Evert's dominance of women's tennis in the late 1970s

"She came in a star and left a star."
Mike Lupica

"She played tennis the way an orchestra plays Beethoven, deftly, lovingly, but with intense concentration on the notes."
Jim Murray

"She knocked everybody out at long range, like the USS *Missouri*."
Jim Murray

"She played with the bored detachment of a pro giving a lesson to an old dowager."
Jim Murray

"I think she should have a nice long honeymoon—say, five years."
JoAnne Russell, before Evert's marriage to John Lloyd

"Even if Chris had to play the match with a cast on her leg."
JoAnne Russell, on how she would do anything to get a victory over Evert

CLAY COURTS

"I'm the only guy in the world who looks like he's playing on clay when I'm on a hard court."
Johan Kriek

"The customers get more for their money on clay. I always felt that at Forest Hills I was gypping them because the points were over quickly."
Rod Laver, on playing the U.S. Open on grass

CLOTHES HORSE

"Obviously—you are."
Andre Agassi, asked by a reporter if he was aware his shorts were see-through

"I overheard a conversation between two girls. One said, 'Hasn't Austin got hairy legs?' Her friend replied, 'What did you expect, feathers?'"

> *Bunny Austin, on being the first man to play Wimbledon's Centre Court in shorts*

"I wore this dress today because it's been lucky for me before against Martina. Now it's gotta be burned."

> *Tracy Austin, on losing to Martina while wearing her lucky peach dress*

"If this avalanche of color-saturated logo-mania isn't enough to make us wish for a little bleach and a pair of scissors, we are currently forced to endure the onslaught of spandex."

> *Mr. Blackwell, on tennis fashions in the '90s*

"Backhand fashion."

> *Mr. Blackwell, on naming Billie Jean King one of the five worst dressers of 1973*

"It used to bother me a lot that they didn't write up the tennis. All they wrote about was Gussie's panties."

> *Louise Brough, on the famous lace*
> *panties worn by Gussie Moran at*
> *Wimbledon in 1949*

"The tennis clothing industry exists only because thousands of people regard life as a costume party in which they masquerade as Ivan Lendl or Chris Evert."

> *Bud Collins*

"She's become a Slav to fashion."

> *Kim Cunningham, on Martina*
> *Navratilova's love of clothes*

"He looks like an American to me."

> *Stefan Edberg, on Jim Courier's*
> *appearance in a baseball cap and an*
> *untucked shirt*

"Tinling's dresses seem designed to keep everyone's eyes off the ball."

> *Louis Greis, Wimbledon official, on*
> *the controversial dresses of Ted*
> *Tinling*

"Our life is showering and changing. I change clothes five times a day and wash my hair every day. It's a tough role to play, so you don't see many femmes fatales in tennis dresses."

Billie Jean King

"Is that where you'd like to have your underwear?"

Gussie Moran, to Ted Tinling, who told her she should donate her famous lace panties to the Tennis Hall of Fame

"Lotto [clothing sponsor] sent me just four white shirts to play at Wimbledon. I guess they didn't have much confidence in my chances."

Thomas Muster, on losing in the first round of the '94 Wimbledon

"Nothing fits except his head rag and his shoes."

Pam Shriver, on Andre Agassi's baggy shirts and shorts

"For her? What about for me? I designed her outfit."

"Confidence can make the difference between winning and losing. . . . If a woman feels she looks better than her opponent, that is an edge."

Ted Tinling, on the importance of dresses in tennis

"It is almost impossible to comprehend how a yard of lace, added to a player's normal undergarment and barely visible, could cause such a furor."

Ted Tinling, on Gussie Moran's lace panties

"I could never understand tennis players who wore nice dresses but showed dreary garments underneath."

Ted Tinling, on his inspiration for adding lace to Moran's panties

"I have nothing but bad to say. The clothes have no movement of any description. If you go to the ballet, you don't expect to see the dancers in clothes that don't move."

> *Ted Tinling, on traditional tennis clothes*

"The Sugar Plum Fairy of the lot."

> *Ted Tinling, on his love for Chris Evert and the dresses he designed for her*

CLUB PROS

"Try golf. I don't need any more competition."

> *Anand Amritraj, advice to club pros on how to get better*

"Show me a club player with four matching rackets and a leather case and I'll usually show you a loser with an expensive hobby."

> *Vic Braden*

"For the club players to face one of us would be like having Albert Einstein drop in for dinner and try to explain the theory of relativity to me."

Peter Fleming

"When the best player at your club calls you out of the blue and invites you to play tennis, he probably wants to sell you life insurance."

Barry Tarshis, tennis writer

COACHES

"We didn't like each other, but he was a very good competitor. He also had a better car than I did."

Bud Collins, on coaching Abbie
Hoffman at Brandeis in the 1950s

"First of all, my name is not George Steinbrenner."

Martina Navratilova, on her frequent
changes of coaches

"The others are all stupid. They don't have intuition."

Pancho Segura, on other tennis
coaches

"Most teaching pros overteach."
Bill Talbert

"The number of tennis coaches who know what they're doing is maybe five percent."
Ion Tiriac

COLLEGE LIFE

"You know, the powerhouse Boston University."
Bob Green, qualifier who made it to the fourth round of the U.S. Open, asked where he went to college

"I'd go to an event, then return to classes a week behind. It was always like being down 5–2 in the final set."
Mel Purcell, on playing for his college tennis team

"He is to tennis what snow is to the winter Olympics, what pasta is to Italy."

> *Donald Dale Jackson*, Sports Illustrated *writer*

"Bud knows more about tennis than 99.5 percent of the population, but what did he ever do in tennis that would make him know what's happening in the U.S. Open?"

> *John McEnroe*

"Collins is the game's great populist, the kindly gentleman next door, our guy in the broadcast booth."

> *Alexander Wolff*, Sports Illustrated *columnist*

COME FLY WITH ME

"Fear of flying in airplanes for a tennis pro is a worse handicap than shaky nerves."

> *Bud Collins*

"Nancy Richey."

> *Jeff Borowiak, asked if he would*
> *rather play Bjorn Borg or Jimmy*
> *Connors in the finals of a tournament*

"Everybody is fighting for food. The way I like to live costs money, and the guy on the other side is trying to make my money."

> *Jimmy Connors*

"I've bowled maybe 25 times in my entire life, yet every time I went up to the line I expected to knock all the pins down."

> *Billie Jean King*

"Son, where's your opponent playing?"

> *Bill Talbert's father, on Talbert*
> *complaining about the surfaces he*
> *was playing on*

CONFLICT OF INTEREST

"For a newspaper, it would be like having George Steinbrenner cover the Yankees."

> *Phil Mushnick, on Donald Dell's role as commentator, agent, and tour promoter*

"If it's not his client who's playing, maybe he's suing the guy."

> *Phil Mushnick, on Dell*

JIM COURIER

"If we could cut off his head, he'd play really well."

> *Brad Stine, his coach, on stopping Courier's slump*

MARGARET COURT

"She would not serve double faults at 5–0, 40–love, but it was quite possible she would at 5 all, deuce."
Ann Haydon Jones

COURT SIDE

"The Masters court gets faster every year. If I keep qualifying, someday I'll play the Masters on glass."
Guillermo Vilus, on the Grand Prix Masters at Madison Square Garden

DAVIS CUP

"You root for our guys and against them. That's what the Davis Cup is all about."
Andre Agassi, on psyching himself up to beat the nice-guy Swedish team

"What I couldn't understand was why, having just beaten me, they still wanted to kill me."

Jimmy Arias, on having stones thrown at him after the United States lost to Paraguay in the Davis Cup

"I know they definitely speak a different language."

Jay Berger, asked what he knew about the Mexican team the United States was playing in the Davis Cup

"At the start, the middle, and the end."

Ricardo Cano, asked if he was nervous playing a vital match for Argentina against Dick Stockton of the United States in Davis Cup competition

"You have to congratulate the Americans. They did everything to lose and they succeeded."

Guy Forget, after the U.S. team played poorly in losing in the first round of the '93 Davis Cup

"I wasn't so upset the other day when a letter came addressed to 'Dave the Dope.' That's the privilege of all sports fans, but how did the post office know where to deliver the mail?"

Dave Freed, captain of some bad
U.S. Davis Cup teams

"If they want somebody who is going to suck up to the suits, they're never going to give it to me."

John McEnroe, on his prospects for
being named U.S. Davis Cup captain

"Usually, we have some problems with spectators. We don't get any."

Veli Paloheimo, on a big crowd of
spectators causing problems in
Finland during Davis Cup
competition

"I hope they never get that desperate."

Richey Reneberg, asked if he would
consider playing in U.S. Davis Cup
singles

"Americans are our vitamins. We wash them down with beer."

> *Fred Stolle, on Davis Cup competition against the United States*

DEATH WATCH

"Tennis is not a matter of life and death. It's more important than that."

> *David Dinkins, former New York City mayor*

"We are all going to die, rich or poor, and I prefer to die in good health."

> *Beppe Merio, tennis pro from the mid-1950s*

DEFAULT

"I must have bad breath or something, because no one wants to play me."

> *Mark Edmondson, after two players in a row defaulted against him*

"I've been the underdog before. I've also been the overdog a few times. Pretty soon, I may be a between dog."

> *Jimmy Connors*

"I talk to them every day. I must, every day and night. I call and they tell me, 'We miss you.'"

> *Steffi Graf, on her German shepherd puppies*

"Finding my dog Yoney when he got lost in L.A. That's the happiest I've been all year."

> *Martina Navratilova, asked to name the highlight of her amazing 1986 season*

DOUBLES

"It's kind of like arriving for dessert."

> *Mary Carillo, on being asked to play doubles and giving up singles*

"Nastase calls me an SOB every time I miss a shot. Arthur says, 'Come on, Jimmy.' I don't know if I can adjust."

> *Jimmy Connors, on changing doubles partners from Ilie Nastase to Arthur Ashe*

"Doubles is sort of a handsome stepchild. It is often more exciting than singles, with longer rallies and more strategy, and most of the spectators who are playing the game are more attuned to doubles."

> *Frank Deford*

"The big goon who plays doubles with John McEnroe."

> *Peter Fleming, asked what his legacy to tennis will be*

"The doubs [doubles] got to be a 99 percent lock if the other poor bastards had to play us after Junior [McEnroe] had lost."

> *Peter Fleming*

"Are you sure you're feeling OK?"

> *Mima Jausovec, when Tracy Austin asked her to be her doubles partner*

"Singles is work and doubles is play."
Gene Mayer

"This may be the first time in their career that these two have actually been separated."
Gene Scott, introducing the legendary doubles team of Frew McMillan and Bob Hewitt separately during Hall of Fame ceremonies

"Playing doubles is like playing a Stradivarius. Playing singles is like playing a plain old violin."
Sherwood Stewart

"People enjoy doubles more than singles because they have to do less work, have a partner to blame for defeat, and have someone to listen to their gripes as they play."
Bill Tilden

"Paul always complains I don't watch the matches. Well, today I watched the whole match."
Cristo Van Rensburg, after beating doubles partner Paul Annacone in singles

"Two weeks ago I win another car here in America and now I go to California and maybe I win three more. I think I open a garage in Romania."
Ilie Nastase

"It's just as well that I won, because if Jennifer Capriati won, she couldn't drive it anyway."
Martina Navratilova, on beating
14-year-old Capriati in a tournament
in which the winner received a car

"If you drive a Porsche or Mercedes at 17, what the heck will you have left to drive when you're 30?"
Pam Shriver

"I still don't have enough money for a Mercedes."
Natalia Zvereva, on her winnings of
over $515,000, much of which was
taken away by the Soviet Federation

STEFAN EDBERG

"I felt like I was playing Sweden in the Davis Cup."
> *Goran Ivanisevic, on playing Edberg in the quarterfinals of his last U.S. Open*

"People say he's always had problems playing the Open, but I think he's won two times there. I would love to have those problems."
> *Goran Ivanisevic, on Edberg and the U.S. Open*

"There's got to be something that gets this guy excited—mud wrestling or something?"
> *Pat Summerall*

EDUCATION

"It happened, like, 2,000 years ago and has nothing to do with what I have to do now."
> *Jennifer Capriati, on studying history in school*

"It was kind of like going to high school, college, and getting a master's all in one week."

> *Chip Hooper, on making it from*
> *qualifying rounds to semifinals of*
> *the U.S. Pro Indoor Tournament*

EGO

"Genius."

> *Eddie Dibbs, asked what one word*
> *best describes him*

"When I'm determined, I'm still the best."

> *Chris Evert, on beating Hana*
> *Mandlikova in the '81 Wimbledon*
> *finals*

EMMO

"Emmo closed more bars and practice courts than anybody I've ever met."

> *Arthur Ashe, on Roy Emerson's*
> *ability to party late into the night*
> *and be the first one at the practice*
> *court in the morning*

ENDORSEMENTS

"A player like Bjorn Borg, who makes in excess of $2 million a year in endorsements, looks like one of those guys who used to walk around town with sandwich boards."

> *Jack Kramer, on players who wear*
> *tennis outfits bearing all the brand*
> *names of their endorsements*

EXHIBITIONS

"If you're paid before you walk on the court, what's the point in playing as if your life depended on it?"

Arthur Ashe, on exhibitions in which the players are paid beforehand

"An exhibition is fun. I fight my guts out against Bjorn. When we play, it's never an exhibition. It's death."

Jimmy Connors, on playing Bjorn Borg in exhibitions

"This is not a show like Billie Jean and Bobby. This is Tyson fighting Holyfield. This is war."

Jimmy Connors, on his match against Martina Navratilova in Las Vegas

"It's like Willie Mays playing on Tuesday and Saturday and then going off to do home-run derby on the other days."

Jack Kramer, on stars who play lots of exhibitions

"Then, the handicap was Riggs's age. Here, we're both old."

> *Martina Navratilova, on comparing the Battle of the Sexes to her exhibition against Connors*

"A Bust in the Dust."

> *Mark Preston,* Tennis *magazine columnist, on Connors beating Navratilova in a boring Las Vegas exhibition, 7–5, 6–2*

"It was worth the price of admission, which in my case was free."

> *Pat Sajak, on the exhibition between Navratilova and Connors*

FANS

"Every time he towels off, it's like the Benny Hill show."

> *Paul Annacone, on Agassi's wild fans*

"To the average sports fan, tennis is played by pampered, insolent children, run by overtanned businessmen, and governed by quarrelsome organizations."

Sally Jenkins, sportswriter

"When you go to a sporting event, wouldn't you rather have it be like a chaotic rock 'n' roll atmosphere than a library?"

Murphy Jensen, urging more fan participation in tennis

"Americans bother you and Europeans stare at you. I don't know which is worse."

Billie Jean King, on fans

"I like demonstrative crowds. People who pay their hard-earned money for a ticket ought to be able to make noise."

Billie Jean King

"We should urge fans to scream or boo if they like, just like in baseball or football. The sport has too much stuffiness and protocol. It needs more pizzazz."

Billie Jean King

"They don't realize all the work that's behind a good shot, and that your performance generally reflects how much practice has gone into it."

Billie Jean King, on fans

"They clap for you the same in the finals as they do for you in the first round."

Hana Mandlikova, on British fans

"That might have been why I didn't play well. I'm not used to being clapped for by the fans."

John McEnroe, on getting cheers before losing to Bjorn Borg in an exhibition

"I probably don't sign any more autographs than before. It's just that people recognize me now when I sign them."

Mikael Pernfors, after winning the Canadian Open

"When you play a guy from the host country, you know the fans are going to be behind him. When I'm playing in the States, I think the fans are more concerned about beer and hot dogs."

Pete Sampras

"I can stand crowds only when I am working in front of them, but then I love them."
Bill Tilden

FICKLE FINGER OF FATE

"I think Connors wins the Finger Award now. I think he's the champion. I can't even win that anymore."

Ilie Nastase, during a slump so severe that he refrained from even using the middle finger

"Actually it was the U.S. that spoiled me. You gave me money and everything. You also taught me to give the sign."

Ilie Nastase, on using the middle finger

"If you had been able to amputate this years ago, maybe I'd have two million more in the bank."

Ilie Nastase, to his doctor, on his famous middle finger

FINES AND SUSPENSIONS

"Jim Courier cursed at the official at the Australian
Open . . . and he only gets fined $1,000. I think
I'm in the wrong sport. Maybe I'll take up tennis."
Charles Barkley

"I feel pretty good about it. I needed a break. It
gave me a chance to go down to Florida, see a
fight in Vegas, and spend a couple of days in L.A."
*Vitas Gerulaitis, on being suspended
for three weeks*

"I swear in Czechoslovakian—that way they don't
fine me."
*Ivan Lendl, on speaking six
languages but cursing only in Czech*

FOOD FOR THOUGHT

"Did you ever see how fast chickens run?"
*Alberto Berasategui, on why he eats
chicken before matches*

"I can't stand to sit still for an hour or two-hour meal. It makes me crazy to sit in the same place that long."

Jimmy Connors, on why he likes
fast food

"I think they miss Wendy's and McDonald's. I think they are used to more greasy foods. They miss the grease."

Paul Haarhuis, of the Netherlands,
on why Americans think European
food is awful

"There is no food I do not like."

Eric Korita, tennis pro, on the
difficulty of losing 40 pounds

"No, I prefer the Häagen-Dazs diet."

John McEnroe, asked if he used the
Haas diet, made famous by Martina
Navratilova

"I certainly don't think my match is a bigger story than Northwestern getting to the Rose Bowl last year."

Todd Martin, a Northwestern grad, playing down the significance of beating Great Britain's Tim Henman in the '96 Wimbledon quarterfinals

"It's a shame that Super Bowl losers skulk off the field. That doesn't happen in tennis at Wimbledon or the U.S. Open. The runner-up gets a lot of applause too."

Bill Walsh

"O.J. talks about his tennis game the way a new golfer talks about his best round."

Bill Walsh, on playing tennis with O. J. Simpson in the early 1980s

FOOTWEAR

"Dad, did they name the shoe after you or were you named after the shoe?"

> *Trevor Smith, young son of Stan Smith, on Smith's line of Adidas sneakers*

FRENCH OPEN

"Last year I had plane reservations made before every match. This year I brought two weeks' worth of socks."

> *Andre Agassi, in 1990, on his newfound resolve to win the French Open*

"Some people don't realize that this is the Borg invitational. They think they can actually win this thing. What a joke."

> *Vic Amaya, on Bjorn Borg's mastery of the French Open*

"A day at the French Open can mirror a lifetime's hope and frustrating beauty and pathos, pleasure and pain."

Rex Bellamy, London Times
columnist

"A knapsack full of bricks."

*Michael Chang, describing the
pressure he felt after winning the '89
French Open*

"Clang Chang and Ding Dong, the witchery of Roland Garros was dead after a 34-year hexing of American men."

*Bud Collins, on the 17-year-old
Chang's French Open win*

"It was like facing the Niekro brothers out there."

*Jim Courier, on the effect of windy
conditions in the '91 French Open
finals*

"It is like running on marbles."

*Stan Smith, on the clay courts at the
French Open*

"If tennis tournaments could be characterized as art forms, the French Open would be an Impressionist painting."

Sam Toperoff, writer

"It's just like a shortstop who can play on grass and not on Astroturf."

Tony Trabert, explaining why Americans are not able to play well on clay at the French Open

FRIENDSHIP

"He's moving into a Holiday Inn tonight."

Sammy Giammalva, on inviting Ramesh Krishnan to stay at his house for a tournament, only to see Krishnan beat him in the first round

"He has beaten me five times already, so I've been enough of a friend to him."

Aaron Krickstein, on playing good friend Jimmy Connors

"Clerc and I were very good friends in years gone by. A couple of weeks ago, we were not so good friends. Now we're good friends again, but not as good as we used to be."

Guillermo Vilas, on losing two straight finals to fellow Argentinean Jose-Luis Clerc

GAMBLIN' MAN

"It doesn't make a difference how much I win playing tennis. I wind up owing them money."

Eddie Dibbs, on refusing to play any more tournaments in Las Vegas

"I hope it was a small house."

Conchita Martinez, told during the 1993 Wimbledon that someone had bet the house on her to win at 33–1 odds

"The exercise is difficult and my shoulder was tired. The good thing was my wallet was obviously empty, so it wasn't that heavy anymore."

Andrei Medvedev, on losing $1,000 in slot machines in Monte Carlo

"Life is six to five against."
Bill Riordan

GET IN THE ACT

"He should stick to tennis."
John McEnroe, on acting with
Sampras in Pizza Hut commercials

"The player owes the gallery as much as an actor owes the audience."
Bill Tilden, on working hard

GOD BLESS THE USA

"Americans get patriotic when they're outside of America. When you're in America, it's a totally different picture."
Rosie Casals

"When you're a kid you don't know swearwords. I learned all that and the gestures over here."

Ilie Nastase, who blames all his bad habits on living in the United States

GOLF

"In golf, you miss your first three shots and it ruins your whole day. In tennis, it is just love–40."

Peter Burwash, commentator

"You can discuss a tennis match in 20 minutes. But a golf round you go over hole by hole, stroke by stroke, and by the time four recaps are finished the sun is rising on a new day."

Alan King

"There are no bad calls."

Ivan Lendl, on why he loves golf

"I am not playing Wimbledon, because I am allergic to grass."

Ivan Lendl, whose love for golf is well known

"Golf is not a sport—it's an artistic exercise like ballet. You can be a fat slob and still play golf."

John McEnroe

"Why the hell would people love that? I don't know. So Lee Trevino can make some more millions? It's a farce."

John McEnroe, on the Senior Tour in golf

"Is golf really a sport, in all honesty? I thought in a sport you had to run at some point."

John McEnroe

"Tennis is like a wonderful, long-standing relationship with a husband. Golf is a tempestuous, lousy lover; it's totally unpredictable, a constant surprise."

Dinah Shore

"Golf is like tennis. The game doesn't really start until the serves get in."

Peter Thomson, pro golfer

"My short game in golf is bad, but it's pretty good in tennis."

Wendy Turnbull, on her ability to
dink the ball over the net

EVONNE GOOLAGONG

"Evonne is one of a kind. She rolls through life as easily as she sweats around a tennis match."

Roger Cawley, her husband

"Evonne doesn't have to see the ball. She hits by radar."

Patti Hogan, after being beaten by
Goolagong in a poorly lit arena

"Evonne flows. She doesn't run like the rest of us. She flows."

Bob Lansdorp, Tracy Austin's coach

"Fraulein Forehand."
Bud Collins

"Well, she's got two sides—her backhand side and suicide."
Cliff Drysdale, on Graf's legendary forehand

"I felt so rushed by Steffi. During points, between points, always. It just feels like she's all over you. Her pace is a little frightening."
Jo Durie

"Ninety-eight percent of the girls are scared to death to play her."
Patty Fendick

"Graf in an iron lung could still take most players into a three-set tiebreaker."
Jim Murray

"There's a new natural law in the universe, as undeniable as gravity: Steffi Graf cannot be stopped."

> *S. L. Price,* Sports Illustrated *columnist*

"With someone like Arantxa or Monica, there's just not quite the same oppressiveness as Graf."

> *Chanda Rubin*

"Walking out there."

> *Pam Shriver, asked to identify the turning point of the match after being crushed by Graf at Wimbledon*

GRAND SLAMS

"Many people say to me that it was easier for a player to win the Grand Slam in my day. I always reply, 'Well, if that is so, why couldn't someone else do it?'"

> *Don Budge*

"It doesn't suck."

*Jim Courier, asked how he felt
making the quarterfinals of a major
tournament for the first time*

"At my age, you don't get many chances for big
wins in the Grand Slams. You've got to make the
most of them."

*Pancho Gonzales, at age 40, after
losing at the 1968 U.S. Open*

"It's not even close. And anyone who tries to tell
you differently is a liar."

*Pancho Gonzales, asked if there was
a difference between the Grand
Slams and other tournaments*

"Everyone is playing for a piece of history. . . . The
Grand Slams never seem to die."

Jack Kramer

"After my first Grand Slam in 1962, I got a cable
from Charlie. It was like all of the rest. All it said
was, 'Do it again.'"

*Rod Laver, on his coach, Charlie
Hollis*

"Any other tournament is just another week of playing tennis."

Ivan Lendl, on the significance of Wimbledon, the U.S. Open, and the French Open

"What fans remember is who wins the Grand Slams. They're not really interested in who won the Lebanon Open or anything. It's the same with golf—who won the Masters or the U.S. Open."
Pete Sampras

GRASS IS GREENER

"Grass-court tennis is rather like watching a dachshund get up. It is impressive, but after five minutes, continuing to watch becomes tedious."
Rex Bellamy

"You can't play on grass if there's no oxygen."
Pat Cash, on why he supports environmental causes

"Got to let one rest and be fertilized while I'm using the other."

> *Bill Cosby, on why he has two grass courts at his house*

"Today."

> *Magnus Gustafsson, clay-court specialist, after his defeat of No. 11 Wimbledon seed Wayne Ferreira, asked when he became a grass-court specialist*

"Grass is for cows."

> *Jan Kodes, on his disdain for grass*

"Sometimes on grass I could lose two sets to my grandmother."

> *Ivan Lendl*

"Grass? Give me a bucket of balls and a sand wedge. Sure, I like grass."

> *Ivan Lendl, on claims he doesn't like to play on grass*

GREAT EXPECTATIONS

"I wish I'd been a really great tennis player."
> *Marilyn Horne, famous opera singer,*
> *on any regrets in her life*

"My volley is blah. I'm a dead elephant on the court. My serve has no sting and I am confused. Other than that, I'm a fine player."
> *Mona Schallau, touring pro*

GREAT EXPECTORATIONS

"Everybody has their habits. I would like to stay quiet, never swear, never spit, and serve 120 aces. But that's just not reality."
> *Boris Becker, on being reprimanded*
> *for spitting too much at the '92*
> *Wimbledon*

GRUNTS AND GROANS

"Very loud."

> Andre Agassi, asked how he thought
> Thomas Muster, a loud grunter,
> would play in an upcoming
> tournament

"Personally, I only grunt when I get a bad call."
> Mary Carillo

"Seles's grunt has a lot more backswing and a
better follow-through."

> Mary Carillo, on the difference
> between the grunts of Monica Seles
> and Jennifer Capriati

"The Donna Summer of tennis."

> Bud Collins, on loud grunter Virginia
> Ruzici

"I was at a boys' tournament in Ocala where nine matches were going on at a time, and it sounded like a pigsty."

> *Bobby Curtis, Florida tennis*
> *coordinator, on the grunting at a*
> *juniors tournament*

"If I wanted my athletes quiet, I'd go watch chess."

> *Mike Downey, L.A. Times columnist,*
> *defending the grunts of Monica Seles*

"Without grunting, she was Rapunzel without the hair, Streisand without the nose."

> *Curry Kirkpatrick, on Seles not*
> *grunting in the '92 Wimbledon final*
> *and losing decisively to Graf*

"The day the Grunter beat the Grannie."

> *London Daily Mail, on Seles beating*
> *Navratilova in the '92 Wimbledon*
> *semifinals*

"It's like someone's hitting me."

> *Monica Seles, describing her grunts*

"It sounds like she's wringing the neck of a Christmas goose."

Ted Tinling, on Seles's grunts

"These days people don't come to see him play. They come to hear him play."

Julie Welch, reporter, on the grunts of Jimmy Connors

GULLIKSON BROTHERS

"No one beats two Gulliksons in a row at Wimbledon."

Tim Gullikson, following his defeat of John McEnroe at Wimbledon soon after McEnroe had beaten Tim's brother Tom

"He is without a doubt one of the uglier guys on the tour."

Tom Gullikson, on his identical twin brother Tim

"Who is this Gullikson guy? Two weeks ago, he beat me playing with his right hand. Now he beat me with his left."

> *Karl Meiler, on losing to right-handed Tom and, two weeks later, to left-handed Tim*

GYMNASTICS

"In tennis, you can never be perfect. You always miss a shot somewhere. And that frustrates me."

> *Bonnie Gadusek, former gymnast turned tennis player, comparing the two sports*

HAIR IT IS

"My body hair is now secondary to tennis."

> *Andre Agassi, on his new devotion to tennis*

"Yeah, I have less hair now."

John McEnroe, in 1984, asked how he had changed from his first appearance at Wimbledon in 1977

"I used to have brown hair."

John McEnroe Sr., gray-haired father, asked how he kept his cool during his sons' matches

"Just call me Madonna."

Monica Seles, on her new short hairstyle

"Somebody reminded me my head would get pretty sunburned."

Monica Seles, on deciding not to shave her head

"Nobody. After a shower, I just put my finger in a light socket."

Roscoe Tanner, asked who combed his Afro hairstyle

HALL OF FAME

"They don't induct you because of your temper. They induct you because of what you did. If they inducted by personality, I'd be the first one not to be inducted, that's for sure."

> *Ilie Nastase, on being elected to the Tennis Hall of Fame*

HEIGHT REPORT

"Short girls who take all the tall guys."

> *Lindsay Davenport, 6'1", on what annoys her*

"Dibbs drives it while sitting on a phone book."

> *Brian Gottfried, on how the 5'7" Dibbs was going to drive his new Cadillac*

"My whole family is short, so tennis is a good sport for us because we're low to the ground."

> *Dustin Hoffman*

HUNKS

"She has trouble keeping her eyes on the ball."
John Bassett, on daughter Carling
playing mixed doubles with
handsome Vince Van Patten

"I hope in about eight years, I will be receiving the same cup from another handsome young tennis player."
Richard Krajicek, on presenting an
honorary trophy to the retiring
Stefan Edberg

HUSTLER

"When a player you're meeting in a tournament for the first time tells you he plays tennis for the fun of it, request a linesman."
Barry Tarshis, Tennis *magazine*
writer

"No matter how hot it gets, it never melts."
> *Anonymous, on the chocolate bar*
> *named after Bjorn Borg*

"My life really operates in two separate sections—
tennis and all the other stuff."
> *Bjorn Borg*

"For Borg that's as believable as Neil Simon writing
four plays without a laugh, or Arthur Miller
writing four of them without a cry."
> *Bud Collins, on Borg losing four*
> *tournaments in a row*

"Pursuing that son of a bitch Bjorn Borg to the
ends of the earth."
> *Jimmy Connors, asked to name his*
> *tennis goals*

"Some days he hardly misses a ball. You have to be
mentally tough, tell yourself you'll hit a million
back, and run after everything—and even then you
might not get a set."
> *Eddie Dibbs*

"Cheering for him is like cheering for a steamroller."

> *Ray Fitzgerald*, Boston Globe
> *columnist*

"There's the rest of us. Then there's Bjorn."

> *Vitas Gerulaitis*

"Who knows what kind of miracle he is?"

> *Jack Kramer*

"I learned a lot out there playing Borg. And one of the big things I learned is I have a long way to go before I'm as good as that guy."

> *Andy Luechesi, after losing to Borg*

"He forces you to make so many great shots. I don't know if it's humanly possible to beat him anymore."

> *Gene Mayer, on Borg*

"Individuals are entitled to react in their own ways to a stressful situation. And to me, Bjorn's way is more of an aberration than John's."

> *John McEnroe Sr., on Borg's stoic demeanor*

"I have no idea how people beat him. I don't see how they win games."
Terry Moor

"And I was told his weakness was against left-handers."
Terry Moor, left-hander who lost to Borg, 6–0, 6–0, 6–1

"He is playing on another planet."
Ilie Nastase

"He's almost a perfect tennis machine, because he never stopped oiling his parts."
John Newcombe

INCONSISTENCY

"I can hit five winners in a row and then I throw in a couple of real shockers."
Pat Cash

"The only time I show any consistency these days is when I'm making a cup of tea."

Mats Wilander, during a slump

INJURIES

"It's a lot of hard work, a lot of ups and downs. But the highs are so high that they make the lows a lot easier to handle."

Mary Carillo, on her comeback from an injury

"Well, Walter hurt his arm when he fell off an airplane. Fortunately, it was on the ground."

Betsy Cronkite, on why her husband Walter didn't play tennis for several months

"You should never complain about an injury. We believe that if you play, then you aren't injured, and that's that."

Roy Emerson

"I went up like Boris Becker and down like Mort Janklow."

> *Mort Janklow, superagent, on how he*
> *sprained his ankle*

INSULT TO INJURY

"I guess she should be cocky. She beat me three years ago."

> *Chris Evert, on Hana Mandlikova*
> *saying that Evert was past her prime*

"It was easier than it looked."

> *John McEnroe, after beating Vijay*
> *Amritraj, 6–1, 6–2, 6–1*

"I don't rise to the occasion against lesser players."

> *Pam Shriver, after she lost to*
> *Wendy Turnbull*

GORAN IVANISEVIC

"Awesome Lefticity."
>*Mary Carillo*

"Great balls of fire."
>*Bud Collins, on his serve*

"Some guy who came from another planet."
>*Goran Ivanisevic, describing himself*
>*after watching videos from earlier in*
>*his career*

JENSEN BROTHERS

"It's doing all the stuff you think you're too cool to do."
>*Luke Jensen, defining Jensenism*

"He's the one who gets the bomb-sniffing dogs at airports because he looks like a drug dealer. But he's the responsible one."
>*Murphy Jensen, on brother Luke*

"He'd beat me in a wheelchair if he could."
Andre Agassi, on Connors's
competitive nature

"Jimmy will be showing up and doing something when he's 50."
Arthur Ashe

"He has one weakness. He can never say his opponent played well. That's why it feels good to beat him and that's why other players would rather beat him than any other player."
Bjorn Borg

"I couldn't consider his age. The guy is Jimmy Connors. We all know how he is, because of who he is."
Michael Chang, after playing him at the 1989 French Open, when Connors was 38

"As though every match was life and death, as if he were being paid on the basis of intensity, selling his guts down to the last hostile drop."

Bud Collins

"If Connors's heart pumped oil, he'd be richer, richer than he is now."

Bud Collins

"In Flushing Meadows, people are so inspired by a 145-pound man doing a war dance that they cheer wildly when his opponent double-faults."

Bud Collins, describing Connors at the U.S. Open

"At 36, you just put one foot in front of the other and hope for the best."

Jimmy Connors, asked if he was playing mind games with an opponent by walking with a swagger

"I've never seen anything like that, and I hope I never see anything like that again."

Jimmy Connors, on taking three hours to beat Eliot Teltscher

"He thinks he's Bob Hope, but he's about as funny as bloody Marcus Welby."

Phil Dent, early in Connors's career

"Connors is a killer. He's got timing, guts, he knows just when to come in and dig. He would've made a helluva fighter."

Angelo Dundee, boxing trainer

"I still have to take out the garbage when I go home."

Drew Gitlin, asked how giving Jimmy Connors a tough match at Wimbledon changed his life

"Normally, Borg does not come out and blow you off the court. He just hits a ton of balls and lets you beat yourself. Connors, though, is the ultimate nightmare when he's hot. Connors can kill you."

Gene Mayer, on preferring to play Borg over Connors

"If Jimmy Connors can be as popular now as he is, anyone's got a chance."

John McEnroe, asked if he thought he might be popular in the future

"I don't think I could ever be that phony."
John McEnroe, on Connors's change to a nice-guy image

"I have great admiration for Jimmy Connors. In fact, my name used to be Connors but I changed it for business reasons."
Chi Chi Rodriguez

"Playing Connors is like fighting Joe Frazier. The guy's always coming at you. He never lets up."
Dick Stockton

JOB HUNT

"It's not like working for a living."
Bud Collins, on announcing

"Except for tennis, I would have been a bag boy in the A & P supermarket."
Eddie Dibbs

"When I was growing up I wanted to be a
neurosurgeon, and even though some people think
I haven't done much since I turned pro, I'd have to
be a damn good surgeon to make what I'm
making."

Kathy Horvath

JUSTICE IS SERVED

"Tennis is like a lawsuit—activity from across the
court is surprising."

Anonymous

"That was one time when my integrity triumphed
over my judgment."

*Antonin Scalia, Supreme Court
justice, on defeating Senator Howard
Metzenbaum in tennis before the
Senate confirmed his appointment to
the bench*

KEEPING SCORE

"Deuce is used so you don't have to count so high."

Bill Cosby

"I can't subscribe to that old cliché that it is not whether you win or lose, but how you play the game. In that case, why keep score?"

Donald Dell

KILLER INSTINCT

"I was an animal early in my career. . . . It was like I had rabies. I've bitten a lot of people along the way, and that's the way I wanted it."

Jimmy Connors

"When you get an opponent down, slam the door on him by going with your best strokes."

Jimmy Connors

"I guess if looks could kill, I would have killed a number of people."

Nancy Richey, on her looks of deep concentration

"A killer with the heart of a lion."

Pancho Segura, on Jimmy Connors

KNOCKOUTS

"If you screw up in tennis, it's 15–love. If you screw up in boxing, it's your ass, darling."

Tex Cobb

"Tennis may have elite origins, but its closest cousin in sports is the most elemental, boxing: two people banging it out until one has punched the other into submission."

Bud Collins

"It's a lot harder than tennis. If I make a mistake, it's like 0–15. In boxing, you let your head down once and then you're in the hospital."

Andrea Jaeger, comparing boxing to tennis

"It's not like I'm a punch-drunk fighter who had too many fights. In tennis, we fight over a net, so we never get hurt like a boxer. I have plenty left."
> *John McEnroe, asked when he was going to retire*

"Nobody ever bleeds on your tuxedo."
> *Barry Tompkins, asked how covering Wimbledon for HBO differs from covering boxing*

LAND DOWN UNDER

"The carriage of thoroughbreds."
> *Allison Danzig, on the great Australian tennis teams*

"If America is the bankroll, Britain the mother, Australia is the conscience of tennis."
> *Frank Deford*

"There was one main street. If you blinked, you missed it."
> *Roy Emerson, on his hometown*

"Australians can't stand a pain in the ass. . . . If you don't treat your mates right or conduct yourself properly, nobody wants to have anything to do with you."

Roy Emerson

"I don't know, mate. You'll have to ask Hop."

Neale Fraser, asked what he thought of the weather at a time when Coach Harry Hopman wouldn't let players speak to the press

"I'll be honest. Beer and women hurt us a lot."

Rod Frawley, on why many of the recent Australian tennis players did not live up to expectations

TAPPY LARSEN

"Of all the players I have known, Art Larsen leads the parade of weirdos by a good margin."

Vic Seixas

HENRI LECONTE

"He plays like all three musketeers at once."
Simon Barnes, London Times, *on Leconte's frenetic style of play*

IVAN LENDL

"The more boring the event, the more he thrives."
Pete Axthelm, sports columnist

"He grabs you and shakes you and keeps shaking."
Jim Courier

"You must have fun in mixed. Ivan, you know, is not really fun."
Hana Mandlikova, asked why she didn't play mixed doubles with her fellow Czech

"I've got more talent in my pinkie than Lendl has in his whole body."
John McEnroe

"Nobody gives a damn about Lendl, that's the bottom line. I could have no personality and be more popular than him."

John McEnroe

"A dirty Commie."

John McEnroe

"I think his style of play—just pound every ball—that is why a lot of players are the way they are today. . . . Guys you just throw out there and play great tennis, but no one really cares about."

John McEnroe, on Lendl being the role model for young players

"The French Open sort of put him on the map, like, 'Oh, he's not a total choke artist.'"

John McEnroe, on losing the '84 French Open to Lendl

"Sure, on a given day I could beat him, but it would have to be a day he had food poisoning."

Mel Purcell, after losing to Lendl in less than an hour

SUZANNE LENGLEN

"Lenglen is not set up as any female beauty, but she is beautiful as an athlete when the flaming colors she wears begin to move, a red or orange lightness blows in the wind."

Grantland Rice

LITTLE MO

"I was a strange little girl armed with hate, fear, and a Golden Racket."

Maureen Connolly

"Never did she go out to lose. Her concentration was so tough, she would be down 5–0, 40–love, in the final set and not be beaten."

Shirley Fry

"She could pass you through a needle's eye. That's how great a player she was."

Althea Gibson

"She didn't just beat you—she dispatched you."
Ted Tinling

"The ideal body for a woman tennis player—a
mosquito torso on piano legs."
Ted Tinling

LOSING

"It was a great match. I wish I could have
watched it."

*Vijay Amritraj, after losing in five
sets to Roscoe Tanner*

"The *New York Times* puzzle was tougher."

*Arthur Ashe, making light of his
losing a match to Cliff Richey*

"Every time you win, it diminishes the fear a little
bit. You never really cancel the fear of losing, you
keep challenging it."

Arthur Ashe

"In each of the six, I had a different opponent. So my overall finish is higher than those six."

> *Arthur Ashe, on losing five of six*
> *finals in one year*

"Every day two million Americans play tennis and one million of them lose."

> *Vic Braden*

"I hate to lose more than I love to win. I hate to see the happiness in their face when they beat me."

> *Jimmy Connors*

"When you lose matches, you're more human."

> *Chris Evert, on her ice princess image*

"When you are winning too much, sometimes you think you should never lose again. I am learning to lose."

> *Goran Ivanisevic*

"The best players, I think, are always the ones who remember their losses, because they remember the pain and they hate it."

> *Billie Jean King*

"It's hard not to get down on yourself when you lose every week like I do."
Jay Lapidus

"If you go into a match with the idea that if you lose, you will be a good loser, you are going to be a loser."
Rod Laver

"I got tired, my ears started popping, the rubber came off my tennis shoes, I got a cramp, and I lost one of my contact lenses. Other than that, I was in great shape."
Bob Lutz, after losing to Guillermo Vilas in a World Team Tennis match

"As you get older the pain of losing is greater, and the joy of winning is diminished."
John McEnroe

"When you are talking about pressure, you're talking about losing. I only think about winning."
Barbara Potter

"I know only one way to play—to win. If I lose, then it is nothing."

Ion Tiriac

LOVE AND MARRIAGE

"My uncle always described an unforced error as his first marriage."

Bud Collins

"Tennis is like marrying for money. Love means nothing."

Phyllis Diller

"How much money do you have?"

Steffi Graf, after a fan yelled out, "Will you marry me?"

"It's 40–love one moment and love–40 the next."

Billy Jean King, on why marriage is like tennis

"Our marriage has survived either in spite of or on account of it. We put a clock on our time together. After seven or eight days, we begin to get on each other's nerves."

Larry King, on his marriage to Billie Jean King

LOVE LIFE

"It was strictly a lifestyle kind of thing."

Chris Evert, on not discussing sex during her appearance on The Dr. Ruth Westheimer Show

"If I did as well on the court as I do off the court, I'd be No. 1 by now."

Vitas Gerulaitis

"Unless there's some emotional tie, I'd rather play tennis."

Bianca Jagger, on sex

"I think he was trying to reduce my matrimonial prospects."

> *Buster Mottram, a bachelor, after being hit several times in a certain painful area by Eliot Teltscher during a match*

"I prefer variety in my apparel, my game, and my love life."

> *Barbara Potter, on wearing a yellow and black outfit to the U.S. Open*

THE LUCK OF THE DRAW

"Like my favorite California grapes, your half of the draw is seedless."

> *Arthur Ashe, to Martina Navratilova, before her '89 Wimbledon appearance*

MAC ATTACK

"John has a presence about him that very few people have. Even when he's on the sidelines, the umpire watches the lines better."

> *Andre Agassi, on playing Davis Cup with John McEnroe*

"If you put John McEnroe in a pair of shorts and flip-flops next to Magic Johnson, who's going to guess that Mac is an athlete?"

> *Paul Annacone, on McEnroe's skinny physique*

"John says he only argues when he's positive [about a call]. Maybe he's got bad eyesight."

> *Jimmy Arias*

"Against Connors and Borg you feel like you're being hit with a sledgehammer. But this guy is a stiletto."

> *Arthur Ashe*

"I always said he was a great player. I never said he was a great human being."

> *Boris Becker, after being taunted by*
> *McEnroe during a match*

"If you outfitted Mikhail Baryshnikov with a tennis racquet and sneakers, he might be able to give a reasonable impression of John Patrick McEnroe."
> *Bud Collins*

"He has been the divine demon. He plays racket strings as exquisitely as Isaac Stern fiddles, behaving like that other fiddler—Nero."
> *Bud Collins*

"Knocking McEnroe is about as demanding as finding potholes in Boston streets."
> *Bud Collins*

"Shut up. Grow up. You're a baby. I've got a son your age."

> *Jimmy Connors, as McEnroe was*
> *arguing a line call during one of*
> *their matches*

"I don't know that I changed all that much. They just found somebody worse."

> *Jimmy Connors, asked if his behavior was improving with age*

"Unfortunately, I can only make one speech, because I haven't John's vocabulary."

> *Chris Evert, on McEnroe not showing up for a championship dinner after the '81 Wimbledon*

"Because John McEnroe never played it."

> *Larry Felser, sportswriter, on why so many millions of people love pro football*

"The best doubles team in the world is John McEnroe and whoever he plays with."

> *Peter Fleming, McEnroe's doubles partner*

"He anticipates the shot before you've even thought of it."

> *Bob Green, touring pro*

"McEnroe is so effortless. . . . He's in places he shouldn't be."

Bob Green

"In the locker room, I felt like Gary Gilmore. You just sit waiting for somebody to come get you."

Bob Green, on facing McEnroe in the fourth round of the U.S. Open

"Watching John perform is like visiting a preschool nursery, except that the four-year-olds have a little more class."

International Dull Folks, on naming McEnroe one of the ten dullest Americans

"I'd like to see Mr. McEnroe join the PGA, just so we could kick him out."

Peter Jacobsen, professional golfer

"If Connors was Dutch Schulz, McEnroe was Al Capone."

Mike Lupica

"All these guys say what an honor it is to play me. What they really mean is they want to kick my ass."

John McEnroe, when he was getting close to retirement

"I'm trying to be a good guy, and I'm not that good a guy."

John McEnroe, on attempting to stop his tantrums

"The guy that first gave me the name said he meant it to mean a youngster who was super, but that's not how it turned out."

John McEnroe, on the "Superbrat" nickname

"Let's put it this way. I'd rather get some attention than no attention. If it's bad, that's life."

John McEnroe

"I'm tired of all the stories about temperamental tennis players. What is this, volleyball?"

John McEnroe

"I'll let my racket do the talking."

John McEnroe, on defending his
Wimbledon title in 1984

"Let him play his game—it's a free country. If you eat steak every day, you get bored. With him, you won't get bored."

Ilie Nastase

"I was tired of him hitting so many good shots."

Raul Ramirez, asked if he was tired
of playing McEnroe

"Same strokes. Same twitches. Give him time and he'll light a fire."

Bud Schultz, touring pro, predicting
how McEnroe would act after a
six-month layoff

"If he's the best young player we got, we're in big trouble. He's flimsy."

Pancho Segura, early in McEnroe's
career

MALAPROPS AND FRACTURED SYNTAX

═══════════════════════════════════════

"I really take an invested interest in this match."
Andre Agassi, on facing McEnroe at
Wimbledon

"He's a great front-runner when he gets ahead."
John McEnroe, on Jim Courier

HANA MANDLIKOVA

═══════════════════════════════════════

"Hana can beat any player on any given day, unless
Martina is playing on the same given day."
Carling Bassett, on Hana Mandlikova

"Her outfits are as inconsistent as her game."
Mr. Blackwell

ALICE MARBLE

"What a girl Alice Marble is, with everything the
Venus de Milo has, plus two muscular, bare,
sunburned arms, marvelously efficient."
Arthur Brisbane, columnist for
Hearst papers

MARTINA

"She's like the old Green Bay Packers. You know
exactly what she's going to do, but there isn't a
thing you can do about it."
Arthur Ashe

"What have I learned from playing Martina? I've
learned how to shake her hand at the net."
Bettina Bunge

"A woman who puts the opposition into concrete
sneakers every time."
Bud Collins

"Why don't you go join the men's circuit and leave us alone."

> *Chris Evert, after being destroyed by Navratilova in a match*

"This court is her court."

> *Chris Evert, on Centre Court at Wimbledon*

"Kick her in the shins."

> *Evonne Goolagong, on the best way to beat Navratilova*

"I don't know—maybe break my left arm."

> *Martina Navratilova, asked how she could lose an upcoming match*

"I don't know if they want to see me play great tennis or see me lose so they can say they were there the night I lost."

> *Martina Navratilova, on fans*

"It's like taking a Ferrari to the shop. We're not changing the whole engine."

> *Martina Navratilova, on fine-tuning her game with the help of Tim Gullikson*

"I hope, when I stop, people will think that somehow I mattered."

> *Martina Navratilova*

"She was beside herself—which, come to think of it, would make a great doubles team."

> *Scott Ostler, columnist, on an emotional outburst by Martina*

"Get in 90 percent of your first serves, return every one of her serves, and you might lose 6–4, 6–4."

> *Pam Shriver, on how to best play Martina*

"She seems a freak of nature, the perfect tennis player."

> *Virginia Wade*

CONCHITA MARTINEZ

"Señorita Topspin."
> *Bud Collins*

"She is the woman who doesn't know how to behave at a going-away party."
> *Bud Collins, as Martinez was beating Martina Navratilova in Martina's last Wimbledon final*

TIM MAYOTTE

"Frontline for most of the decade and perennial candidate at Wimbledon, Mayotte has been good only for flushing at Flushing."
> *Bud Collins, on Mayotte's run in the 1989 U.S. Open at Flushing Meadows*

"This taught me a lesson, but I'm not sure what it is."
> *John McEnroe, on losing to Tim Mayotte in a tournament*

"I tell people just to do what I do. Turn the sound off."

> *Bud Collins, on people who don't*
> *like his announcing*

"I tried to explain why one guy won and the other one didn't, and what one guy was trying to do to the other."

> *Allison Danzig, longtime tennis*
> *reporter for the* New York Times

"I wasn't a good newspaperman. You see, I relied on honesty."

> *Harry Hopman, on leaving*
> *newspaper reporting to be a coach*

"I guess I'd become a German shepherd or something—or a journalist, if I wanted to be mean to myself."

> *Ivan Lendl, asked what he would be*
> *if he came back reincarnated*

"I can't rationalize talking to press people, because they're not rational people."
John McEnroe

"I learned I should keep my mouth shut."
Andrei Medvedev, on what he learned from press conferences

"In Czechoslovakia, there is no such thing as freedom of the press. In the United States, there is no such thing as freedom from the press."
Martina Navratilova

"If you cannot live with them, they are going to kill you. If they kill you, you are not strong enough."
Ion Tiriac, on journalists

MENTAL GAME

"I am not the type of player who responds well to a lot of thinking."
Andre Agassi

"Don't think, dear. Just hit."
> *Nick Bollettieri, offering advice to*
> *Mary Pierce*

"All I ever see is my opponent. You could set off dynamite in the next court and I wouldn't notice."
> *Maureen Connolly*

"I attacked my weaker opponents more furiously than any other girl in the history of tennis."
> *Maureen Connolly*

"This was no passing dislike, but a blazing, virulent, powerful, and consuming hate. I believed I could not win without hatred."
> *Maureen Connolly, on her opponents*

"I never keep my mind so well, so long. I have one more day to do that, then I can relax my brain."
> *Goran Ivanisevic, on preparing for*
> *the '92 Wimbledon finals*

"The trouble with me is every match I play against five opponents—umpire, crowd, ball boys, court, and myself. It's no wonder sometimes my mind goes to the beach."

Goran Ivanisevic

"I see one coming and visualize just where I'm going to hit it, and the shot's perfect—and I feel beautiful all over."

Billie Jean King, on making a great shot

"There is not time to think on the tennis court; the less you think, the better off you are."

Jack Kramer

"I tried not to think about it, so I did."

Paul McNamee, at age 32, after facing 15-year-old Michael Chang, asked if the age difference was on his mind during play

"Many fights are won at the weigh-ins, golf rounds at the first tee. The old Yankees used to win World Series games with batting practice."

Jim Murray, on the importance of confidence in tennis

"I just try to concentrate on concentrating."
>   *Martina Navratilova, on the key to*
>   *her success*

"No one hits the ball for you out there or tells you what to do under the pressure of a match. You're out there for two or three hours all alone with no one to tell you what to do but yourself."
>   *Martina Navratilova*

"As soon as I get into tactics, I get into trouble."
>   *Monica Seles, asked to explain her*
>   *tactics in winning tournaments*

"I concentrated so hard I got a headache."
>   *Stan Smith, on winning a hard-*
>   *fought Davis Cup match in 1972*
>   *against Ion Tiriac*

"Sometimes I believe I give up without giving my best. But if I don't give a 100 percent effort, I won't know how really bad I am."
>   *Mats Wilander*

"It's a no-win situation. If you play hard, you're not going to get the reputation as a nice guy, are you? And if you're a nice guy, you're going to lose."
John Alexander

"Friendships and marriages creak under the strain of the game—especially mixed doubles, which can turn into all-out war."
Vic Braden

"You either go to bed with someone or you play tennis with them. But don't do both."
Art Buchwald

"Talk to any marriage counselor and you'll learn that mixed doubles have caused more divorces than mothers-in-law."
Bud Collins

"Is it just another dirty game that should be banned by the Supreme Court?"
Bud Collins, on mixed doubles

"Though cute and athletic, Gadusek has the air of a gun moll, and Panatta has obviously been hitting the fettucine at full throttle. Call them Bonnie and Wide."

> *Curry Kirkpatrick, on the doubles*
> *pairing of Adriano Panatta and*
> *Bonnie Gadusek*

"Mixed doubles are always starting divorces. If you play with your wife, you fight with her. If you play with somebody else, she fights with you."

> *Sidney Woods*

MONEY GAME

"What's a nice Communist like you gonna do with all that money?"

> *Bud Collins, to Ilie Nastase after*
> *Nastase won a tournament*

"I won three Wimbledons in the 1960s and didn't make any money. I've played only three matches this year and have won over $300,000."

> *Billie Jean King*

"They made me an offer I could afford to refuse."

> *Rod Laver, on contract negotiations with the L.A. Strings of World Team Tennis*

"She has nothing to lose. Her father has millions and she doesn't have to worry."

> *Hana Mandlikova, on pressure Carling Bassett would feel playing in the Wimbledon semifinals*

"I would gladly give back a quarter of my prize money every year if I were able just to be left alone."

> *John McEnroe*

"Too much money involved. When not so much money in tennis, not any problems."

> *Ilie Nastase, on why tennis had so many problems in the 1970s*

"The prize money at the U.S. Open and Wimbledon is pathetic. Tennis players are really pulling in next to nothing."

> *Martina Navratilova*

"You read the papers and see the telephone numbers players you've never heard of are playing for today."

Ken Rosewall

MOON BALL

"Tennis courts will have to be rather large."

Isaac Asimov, asked about playing tennis on the moon

GUSSIE MORAN

"If I could put my brain inside yours, you'd be the top player inside a year."

Bill Tilden, to Moran

MOVIES

"When Pancho Gonzales is the best actor in the movie, well, you know you're in trouble."

> *Anonymous, on the movie* Players, *featuring many tennis stars of the 1970s*

"I knew I was nervous when I kept referring to retakes as double faults."

> *Tony Trabert, on his acting debut in the movie* The Outfit

MUSCLES
(KEN ROSEWALL)

"I have no idea how he manages it, but 99 percent of the time he is in perfect position to hit whatever you send back."

> *Arthur Ashe*

"Pity? I've seen people pity Ken Rosewall and lose 6–3 in the fifth."

> *Jimmy Connors, asked if he felt pity toward Rosewall at the 1974 U.S. Open finals, won by Connors, 6–1, 6–0, 6–1*

"Not everybody was for Rosewall. There were eight for me."

> *Jimmy Connors, on the fans at the '74 U.S. Open finals*

"Muscles is always the favorite. It doesn't matter if it's 35s, 45s, or 65s, Muscles is the favorite."

> *Owen Davidson, on the seemingly ageless Rosewall*

"Sometimes I'd like to kick the little bastard. But like everybody, I marvel at him."

> *John Newcombe*

"At Wimbledon, at the 1976 final when I beat him, the only people clapping for me were my wife and my mother-in-law."

> *John Newcombe, on Rosewall's popularity*

"Maximum results with the minimum effort."
Ken Rosewall, on his style

MUSIC TO MY EARS

"I hope it's not bad luck. I had a racehorse named after me, and he was gelded. I hope nothing like that happens to them."
Bud Collins, on a rock group that named itself Bud Collins

"I go to the locker room and the kids have headphones. They say they're listening to ZZ Top. Whatever happened to the Four Tops?"
Jimmy Connors

"All people have a right to enjoy a hobby, but there is a limit—like charging $15 dollars for a show like this."
Mans Ivarsson, Swedish music critic, on Mats Wilander's band

"I have learned to control my temper, my joy or disappointment. Therefore, in my singing, although I am incurably romantic and sentimental, I find it difficult to register on my face things I feel inside."

Alice Marble, on taking up singing after her tennis career

"It's not to be No. 1, although that would probably thrill me. It is to be able to play the piano."

Terry Moor, touring pro, on his major ambition in life

"You can't do either well if you let your mind wander for one little second to anything else."

Luciano Pavarotti, on why tennis is like singing

"That's OK, you ought to see us play tennis."

Michael Stipe, lead singer of R.E.M., on Jim Courier having problems playing guitar with them

"McEnroe's music is like his tennis—loud, screaming. I play music like my tennis, too, not loud, not flashy."

Mats Wilander

"His unflagging energy explodes into virtually every muscular topspinning shot, with sound effects that make Monica Seles seem mute."
Bud Collins

"It wasn't a smooth transfer to No. 1 for Muster. It's more like he's become No. 1 with an asterisk."
Jim Courier, on Muster, most of whose victories had come on clay

"When you go into the ring to play against Muster, you feel like a small moth against a big elephant."
Yevgeny Kafelnikov

"Muster has no respect for limited players, which is odd, since he's limited himself."
Stephen Noteboom, doubles specialist, on Muster, a notorious clay-court specialist

"Thomas and I have played each other since we were 14, and we didn't like each other then. This isn't like soccer—where you have to pass the ball to the other guy."

Horst Skoff, rival of Muster

MY CUP RUNNETH OVER

"My mother will be happy about the cup. She's always asking for a cup, and I bring only money."

Balazs Taroczy, on winning $36,000
and a silver cup in a tournament

NAKED TRUTH

"I couldn't have caused more of a stir if I had walked out there naked."

Gussie Moran, on her lace panties

"I should've taken all my clothes off, because I've won two years in a row."

> *Pete Sampras, after throwing his shirt in the air following his second straight Wimbledon win*

"Tennis should be played only in the long grass in the meadows—and in the nude."

> *George Bernard Shaw*

NAME GAME

"The all-verb final."

> *Mary Carillo, on Sabine Hack playing Mary Pierce in a tournament final*

"Probably not a household name in his own household."

> *Bud Collins, on Neville Godwin, who defeated Boris Becker at the '96 Wimbledon*

"When I win, call me Evert. When I lose, call me Lloyd."

> *Chris Evert, on how she should be*
> *addressed after her marriage to John*
> *Lloyd*

"What can you do when you have a name that sounds like a disease?"

> *Vitas Gerulaitis*

"Everybody thinks my name is Jerry Laitis and they all call me Mr. Laitis."

> *Vitas Gerulaitis*

"My mother wants to get her name in the papers too."

> *Arantxa Sanchez-Vicario, on why she*
> *added the name Vicario to her name*

"Natalia is a passport name, and I always thought it sounded way too official. Natasha is kind of nice and soft and mellow."

> *Natasha Zvereva, on why she*
> *changed her name from Natalia*

"I don't think Nastase could play tennis if he had my emotional makeup. Unless Nastase can emote, he can't play."

Arthur Ashe

"It's about 35 pages long, and about 15 of them are devoted to penalties associated with his behavior."

Jerry Buss, owner of the L.A. Strings, on the team's contract with Nastase

"Ilie has the legs and temperament of a racehorse."

Julie Heldman, TV commentator

"Nastase guarantees you some action, one way or the other."

Jack Kramer, on his popularity

"The only reason he gets away with it is because the officials and tennis directors don't have the strength or will to stop him."

Sandy Mayer

"He's done more for the game than any single player who has ever lived."

John McEnroe

"What irritates me is that the nice guys off the court are usually the ones who try to stab you in the back on court."

John McEnroe, on Nastase

"You just have to make allowances for him, like you would for an Einstein. The man is a genius, and there have to be allowances for that."

Fred McNair

"Take the racket away from Ilie Nastase and you go from Count Dracula to the Count of Monte Cristo, a suave, hand-kissing type, a lover, not a lug."

Jim Murray

"I'm in the business now of making people famous."

Ilie Nastase, on consistently losing to young up-and-coming players

"They don't call me Nasty anymore. They call me Nicely."

Ilie Nastase, on trying to change his image

"I want to play the game inside out and upside down."

Ilie Nastase

"The guy's a pig. He has the manners of a goat."

JoAnne Russell, after Nastase slammed the ball at her in mixed doubles

"I feel sometimes like a dog trainer who has taken his little puppy and taught it everything. Then, just when training is finished, the dog makes a puddle in the middle of the floor."

Ion Tiriac

"He is scared to lose, he is scared to win, he is scared of everything. Nastase does not have a brain; he has a bird fluttering around in his head."

Ion Tiriac

"The guys from Europe like playing outdoors on clay because of the sun and the birds that sing. We don't have birds in New York. We just have honking horns."

> *Vitas Gerulaitis, on why he prefers indoor courts*

"McEnroe has got a lot more talent than I have, but now he doesn't own New York anymore. I got some of the Bronx back."

> *Vitas Gerulaitis, after defeating McEnroe in a Masters tournament at Madison Square Garden*

"My teenage daughter has a new boyfriend. My son just made the basketball team in junior high school. And my wife found a tennis partner she can beat."

> *Lou Holtz, on why it was tough leaving New York*

"I come from the Lower East Side, where the only guys with rackets are hoodlums."

> *Alan King*

"We're overstated with people who do things well, especially in New York. You just walk down the street here and you see five champions of something. Nothing is special here."

> *Gene Mayer, on New Yorkers not appreciating the greatness of McEnroe*

"You travel all over the world and you wind up with a guy from your hometown. I think it's borough genetics."

> *Patty Smyth, on planning to marry fellow Queens resident John McEnroe*

NICE GUYS FINISH FIRST

"I'm trying to kick your ass. In a nice way."

> *Pete Sampras, on his on-court philosophy*

OFFICIALS OF THE GAME

"Let players call their own lines."
Jimmy Connors, on eliminating
disputes about officiating

"Four or five years ago, I probably would have jerked that guy out of the chair. But my son was watching and I didn't want to upset him."
Jimmy Connors, on choosing not to
dispute a bad line call

"I think the general consensus among the guys is that we prefer to get angry at linespeople instead of computers."
Jim Courier, on replacing officials
with electronic lines

"Some of the linesmen are 80 years old. . . . They should be athletes, not grandmothers."
Vitas Gerulaitis, on selecting
linespeople for the U.S. Open

"In football, they're breaking the rules on every play, and nobody gets nearly so worked up about that as they do when some poor linesman blows one call in the third set."

Jack Kramer

"You missed your calling. You should have been an usher."

Sandy Mayer, to John McEnroe, after McEnroe screamed at a fan to shut up and sit down

"I know being a linesman is a thankless job, especially with guys like me around."

John McEnroe

"You go to the Open, you get the same people who were working the Easter Bowl for me when I was 12. . . . It'd be like refs in the NBA doing CYO games in Great Neck."

John McEnroe

"Bumps on a log."

John McEnroe, describing tennis officials at a tournament

"I hate that sound."

John McEnroe, after a linesman said his ball was out

"I'm not paranoid, but that machine knows who I am."

John McEnroe, disagreeing with an electronic line-calling machine

"Mr. Umpire, could you please make another bad call for me?"

John McEnroe, after a bad call

"Words cannot possibly describe how low you are."

John McEnroe, after another bad call

"Grow some hair."

John McEnroe, disagreeing with the call of a bald linesman

"You are the pits of the world."

John McEnroe, after another bad call

"Disgrace to mankind."

John McEnroe, after yet another bad call

"Just because you happen to get angry at a call doesn't mean you're a bad guy."

John McEnroe

"Tennis judges are usually frustrated tennis guys who didn't make it, or old people who want to be around the sport."

John McEnroe

"You might have the linesmen making mistakes, but they don't yell 'out' for no reason at all."

Martina Navratilova, on line judges being replaced by machines

"Naughty boy."

Fred Perry, giving his reaction to linesmen who make bad calls

"It's like hitting a home run that's inches fair, but it's called foul."

Vic Seixas, on tough line calls

TOM OKKER

"What makes Okker's stroke all the more amazing is the fact that he does so many things wrong."

Jack Kramer, on Okker's topspin forehand

OLYMPICS

"They should have more Olympic Games—every four months, I think."

Goran Ivanisevic, after partying his way through the '92 Olympics

"Chang is Mr. Nice Guy—'The Lord this, that, and the other thing.' I don't know why he wouldn't jump to be in the Olympics."

John McEnroe, on Michael Chang not playing in the '96 Olympics for the United States

"I think the millionaire tennis players are the only amateurs here. . . . They are on vacation from capitalism and want only the medal."

Ion Tiriac, on the '88 Olympics

"It would be just another stamp in my passport."

Mats Wilander, on not participating in the '88 Olympics

OVEREXPOSURE

"She was funny. I just hope the next time it happens the woman is under 25."

Boris Becker, on a woman exposing her breasts during a match he was playing

"I know the ATP has been trying to create more interest in the game. But I don't know if this is what they had in mind."

Michael Chang, on Jeff Tarango dropping his pants on the court during a match with Chang

PANCHO

"Pancho is a very even-tempered man. He's always mad."

Anonymous

"Sure, I'm an old man now. When I was the champion, I was the villain. I had both the opponents and the crowd against me. I think I like the change."

Pancho Gonzales, on being a crowd favorite late in his career

"I don't know how, but Pancho always knows where I was going on the court and hit it the other way."

Rod Laver

PARTY ON

"They were the only guys you could play tennis with in the day and drink with at night."

Alan King, explaining why his favorite players were John Newcombe and Rod Laver

"I must have. I remember the bar across the street."

> *Rod Laver, asked if he remembered playing in a tournament in New Jersey*

"I've got a friend who is a nun, and she has a better social life than I have."

> *Wendy Turnbull, on life as a tennis pro*

"I played that late before, but not tennis."

> *Mats Wilander, after playing a match that lasted till two-thirty in the morning*

FRED PERRY

"The most ruthless player who ever walked on a court."

> *Bobby Riggs*

POETRY IN MOTION

"Writing free verse is like playing tennis with the net down."

Robert Frost

POLITICAL FRONT

"The one thing I don't need right now is ulcers."

Arthur Ashe, asked after his heart surgery if he was interested in running for political office

"They're happy to play with a senator—while I'm happy to play with someone good."

John Breaux, senator from Louisiana, on Senate interns who are good tennis players

"He's a very good player. I think he's a much better player than he is a vice president."

Art Buchwald, on George Bush during his tenure as vice president

"The thing you must remember when you play tennis with the Kennedys is that they hate to lose. . . . The safest thing to do if you want to have dinner is to play well but lose."

Art Buchwald

"I've known those two since the mid-'60s, and they're very nice about suffering fools gladly on the court."

George Bush, on playing tennis with John Newcombe and Tony Roche

"A tennis player asked Rudy for advice, and he said, 'Take two and hit to right.' He doesn't understand anything about tennis."

David Dinkins, former mayor of New York, on current mayor Rudolph Giuliani

"People trust their tennis partners—even their opponents."

Karen Feld, syndicated columnist, on why all Washington insiders play tennis with one another

"I stopped doing that because I figured out that they liked the court more than they liked me."

Marlin Fitzwater, press secretary for President Bush, on inviting dates to play tennis on the White House courts

"I need all the help I can get."

Gerald Ford, on adding a graphite racket to his collection

"No, I can beat him already."

Jack Ford, son of President Ford, asked if Chris Evert was giving him tips on how to beat his dad

"I'd be happy to hit one like Ivan Lendl."

Gary Hart, after John McEnroe beat Lendl in the U.S. Open, asked if he would like to be able to hit a volley like McEnroe

"You know what kind of competitor he is? When he beats me, the entire world should know. When I beat him, it's a national secret."

> *Hamilton Jordan, President Carter's chief of staff, on playing the president*

"We're a couple of conservative guys."

> *John McEnroe, asked why he thought Margaret Thatcher enjoyed his matches*

"It's very close, but I'd take Bush. I want him to win because he's a tennis player."

> *Ilie Nastase, on picking George Bush over Michael Dukakis as his presidential choice in 1988*

"I used to play when I was younger, but I don't anymore because I can't get the horse on the court."

> *Ronald Reagan, on preferring horseback riding to tennis*

"I don't think he has to learn anything. . . .
I mean, an actor was the president of the United
States."

*Ion Tiriac, on Ilie Nastase running
for mayor of Bucharest*

PRACTICE

"Heavens no. Everything is ahead of me. I love
tennis. I even love to practice."

*Tracy Austin, at age 17, asked if she
worried about burnout*

"The only way to practice is under a gamelike
situation. Some people are great players at 2:30,
but the match doesn't start until 3:00."

Vic Braden

"I spend about two hours trying to get a court. You
can get a lot of experience doing that."

Art Buchwald, on his practice routine

"In the years I have played tennis, I have looked for a born tennis player, but I have yet to find one."

> *Bill Tilden, on the importance of practice*

"In tennis, fads become forest fires."

> *Ted Tinling, on new practice techniques*

PREGNANT PAUSE

"Normally, one must go to a maternity ward to see pacing like this by a man."

> *Mary Carillo, on Milan Srejber, who walked a great deal between each point*

"I can still beat my husband—but I could beat him when I was nine months pregnant."

> *Chris Evert, on playing her husband, Andy Mill, after their son was first born*

PRESSURE

"There is more pressure in other things—like supporting a family—than playing tennis."

> *Boris Becker, on how pressure in tennis is overrated*

"When I was 18 years old and on my belly in Iwo Jima, I used to comfort myself by thinking, 'Boy, am I lucky not having to deal with the pressure of big-time tennis.'"

> *Abe Lemons, basketball coach, on John McEnroe complaining about the pressure of being ranked No. 1*

RANKINGS

"She looked like the greatest No. 99 since the Great One, Wayne Gretzky."

> *Bud Collins, on No. 99–ranked Gigi Fernandez making it to the Wimbledon semifinals*

"Overseeded."

> *Jimmy Connors, seeded No. 1 at*
> *Wimbledon, asked how he felt going*
> *five sets against Phil Dent early in*
> *the tournament*

"Once you've been No. 1, you can never be satisfied with less."

> *Chris Evert*

"If we weren't No. 1 and 2 in the world, I know we'd be very, very close."

> *Chris Evert, on her friendship with*
> *Martina Navratilova*

"Let's not get ridiculous here."

> *Chris Evert, not playing well after*
> *first being married to John Lloyd,*
> *asked how she would feel if she*
> *were ranked as low as No. 33*

"I have two words to say on that: 'No' and 'comment.' Put them together."

> *Ivan Lendl, on controversy over his*
> *No. 1 ranking*

"I don't look like a No. 1 player. People say to me, 'You don't look like an athlete. You look like a person.'"

Monica Seles

"I'm not sure who I play next, but I'm sure he's ranked above me."

Michael Tebbutt, ranked No. 870 in the world, after beating his first-round opponent

RASH JUDGMENTS

"Tennis has skyrocketed to the top, and now that it's gotten there, nobody knows what to do with it."

Jimmy Connors

"When I first saw Andre at age two or three, I didn't think he was going to be any good."

Pancho Gonzales, on Andre Agassi

"Two or three more years, that's all. . . .With so much money, I think they lose their competitive urge."

> *Pancho Segura, Connors's coach, asked how much longer the 25-year-old Connors would play competitively*

READ ANY GOOD BOOKS LATELY?

"Don't have one. I never read books."

> *Andre Agassi, on his favorite book*

"Yeah, all I need are some books."

> *Jimmy Connors, on suggestions that the two trophies he won in a tournament could serve as bookends*

"I thought it was a pretty good book. It made me look pretty good actually, for the mean SOB I am."

> *Jimmy Connors, on Chris Evert's autobiography*

"It prepares you for the depression after."

Bob Green Jr., after losing to John McEnroe at the U.S. Open, asked if his major in Russian literature helped prepare him for the match

RELIGION

"Don't tell Leonardo that the Holy Land has run out of miracles."

Bud Collins, on Leonardo Lavalle being ranked No. 218 in the world after winning the Tel Aviv Open

RETIREMENT

"One was that I started playing tennis, the other that I stopped doing it."

Bjorn Borg, on his two greatest accomplishments

"Quit asking me about my retirement. If you're pushing me out, I'll stay a lot longer."

Jimmy Connors, on rumors of his retirement

"Why do people keep asking me if I'm going to quit? Did anybody ask Rubinstein when he was going to stop playing the piano?"

Billie Jean King

"You must be joking. With my temper, no kid would be safe."

Ilie Nastase, responding to suggestions that he be a teacher after his retirement

"I like people recognizing me in a restaurant, getting a table when it's crowded. It will bother me for a while when that stops. It's like one day you're famous, and the next day you go to jail."

Ilie Nastase, on his impending retirement

"You talk to any athlete who has been there for a long time, it doesn't matter how much they have won. You want that one more chance."

> *Martina Navratilova, at the end of her career*

"Not at all. I don't enjoy playing guys I know I can't beat."

> *John Newcombe, asked if he missed playing competitive tennis*

"Ever since I started out on the tour, she's supposedly been on her last legs. She must be a centipede. What do they have, 100 legs?"

> *Pam Shriver, on continued rumors of Chris Evert's retirement*

RETURN OF SERVE

"Returning a booming serve is just a matter of confidence."

> *Tappy Larsen*

"You hold that whip when you serve, but you can take the whip for yourself with your return."

Frew McMillan

"If you can return the ball successfully three times in a row, you will probably win the point."

Hazel Hotchkiss Wightman

RISE AND SHINE

"I thought it was a skit from *Saturday Night Live* when I heard about it. I've never ever gotten up at that hour."

John McEnroe, on playing in a final at nine-thirty in the morning

RIVALRIES

"The point is that she is No. 6 in doubles and I'm No. 0."

Tracy Austin, on asking longtime rival Pam Shriver to be her doubles partner

"I know what we do in the next few years is going to be remembered long after we're both six feet underground."

> *Jimmy Connors, on his rivalry with Bjorn Borg*

"Every Dempsey has a Tunney. Every Ali has a Frazier."

> *Mike Estep, Martina Navratilova's coach, on her rivalry with Chris Evert*

"I could play to 90 percent of my potential and still win most of my matches against the other players. With Martina and me, whoever wins has to play 100 percent."

> *Chris Evert*

"I hate to say it, but now it's normal when she beats me. When you get your head knocked against the wall, you can't forget it."

> *Chris Evert, on her rivalry with Martina*

"Watching Connors and McEnroe play was a little bit like watching the Indianapolis 500. You know that a good portion of the crowd was there not to see them play, but to explode."

John Feinstein

"There's no rivalry yet. I've beaten him once, and he's beaten me six times."

John McEnroe, on his early battles with Bjorn Borg

"She kept Martina from swallowing the game whole."

Jim Murray, on Chris Evert's impact

"You brought a lunch when they played. Or a breakfast."

Jim Murray, on several matches between Stefan Edberg and Michael Chang that lasted over four hours

"I don't miss seeing all those backhands going past me when I am at net."

Martina Navratilova, asked if she would miss her rivalry with the recently retired Chris Evert

"The game's Road Runner and Wile E. Coyote."

*Steve Rushkin, on longtime rivals
Steffi Graf and Arantxa Sanchez-
Vicario*

"It's like the *Valdez* oil spill. Oil and water don't
mix, so everyone notices."

*Brad Stine, Jim Courier's former
coach, on the Agassi–Sampras rivalry*

ROCKET ROD

"When Rod goes on one of those tears, it's just
ridiculous. He starts hitting the line, and then he
starts hitting the line harder and harder and
harder. No one can stop him."

*Arthur Ashe, describing Rod Laver
on a roll*

"It looks as though the sport will have to be
opened considerably wider to include angels, highly
trained kangaroos, or something as yet
unenvisaged, before anyone else will be in Laver's
league."

Roy Blount Jr., on Rod Laver

"His left wrist is so strong that he'd knock his own teeth out if he didn't brush them right-handed."
Bud Collins

"If Laver wore a top hat, you'd think he was Mandrake the Magician."
Bud Collins

"This may be like faulting Sophia Loren for having an ingrown toenail."
Bud Collins, on Rod Laver's one weakness being midcourt lobs

"When I make a truly great shot, I look up and thank God. Rod takes his for granted."
John Newcombe

"Talking to Rod Laver is like watching grass grow."
Bill Riordan

"How tough it must have been for him to play his heart out, to reach standards so strong . . . only to be permitted merely an ignominious hurt on the court."

Lance Tingay, after Tony Roche played well but still lost a Wimbledon final to Laver

ROLE MODELS

"Just think of all those people out there. If they see me with a racket in my hand, they say, 'Hey, wait a minute. I can do that.'"

Art Buchwald, on being a role model for tennis

"Kids aren't morons. They don't sit there and say, 'I'm gonna copy McEnroe yelling at umpires.' They love me because they see a personality."

John McEnroe, on being a role model

"Why two? We have royalty every day and we've never lost one yet."

> *Anonymous, on Patricia Nixon Cox*
> *having two bodyguards at the Royal*
> *Box while her dad was President*

"I didn't want to risk the embarrassment, as an American, of seeing an American disgrace our country."

> *Charlton Heston, on refusing to sit in*
> *the Royal Box while John McEnroe*
> *was playing*

ROYALTY

"I don't know if a title is going to make a whole lot of difference in my life. It's something else if you receive something like that, but if you buy a title it cannot be worth that much."

> *Boris Becker, on being outbid for the*
> *title of Lordship of Wimbledon*

"I didn't know who they were. I shouldn't say this, but I was thinking, 'Couldn't they wait till after the changeover?'"

> *Jennifer Capriati, on her '92 match at the Barcelona Olympics being interrupted by the entrance of King Juan Carlos and Queen Sophia*

"The only thing I've noticed is that when I come into the locker room they all bow."

> *Martina Navratilova, asked if her rivals were intimidated by her*

"The title is one which carries a lot of responsibility, and he should not buy it for his own amusement."

> *Norman Plastow, chairman of the Wimbledon Society, on Boris Becker trying to buy the title Lordship of Wimbledon*

PETE SAMPRAS

"Both of us would be miserable if we had to live like the other one."

> *Andre Agassi*

"He doesn't cook well."

> *Michael Chang, asked if Sampras*
> *had any weaknesses*

"You need an ax instead of a racket to break his serve."

> *Bud Collins*

"He offers more shots than a bartending octopus or an allergist."

> *Bud Collins*

"He could play well on nails."

> *Jim Courier, asked if he liked*
> *Sampras's chances in a match to be*
> *played on clay*

"I would take him on my side for one-on-one tennis, two-on-two, three-on-three, any surface. I would take him for golf."

> *Tom Gullikson*

"Friends don't let friends play Pete Sampras in Grand Slam finals."

> *John Jeansonne, Newsday columnist, on Sampras's record of 8–2 in Grand Slam finals*

ARANTXA SANCHEZ–VICARIO

"The Barcelona Bumblebee."
> *Bud Collins*

SCHOOL DAYS

"If I didn't do my homework, what would I say, 'My dog ate it?'"

> *Tracy Austin, explaining why she never skipped her homework while playing on the pro tour*

"They know I'm not ditching."

> *Lindsay Davenport, asked if her teachers get angry when she misses school while playing on the pro tour*

"I hate homework."

> *Peanut Louie, on why she turned pro at age 18*

"I love to go out there and hit. I just can't restrain myself. If you can't have fun, you might as well go to school."

> *Anne Smith, on her love for hitting the ball*

MONICA SELES

"It's Steffi's forehand off both sides."

> *Chris Evert, on Monica's incredible forehand and backhand*

"I'd rather be playing Monica Seles."

> *Martina Navratilova, on being forced to testify during the Judy Nelson palimony suit*

SENIOR TOUR

"I want this [Senior Tour] to succeed big time. I want a job when I'm 35."

> *Jim Courier, at age 21, on the*
> *proposed Senior Tour*

SERVES

"Watch Schultz-McCarthy serve and you want to call up the Army and suggest that they name their next cannon Big Brenda."

> *Peter Bodo,* Tennis *magazine, on the*
> *awesome serve of Brenda Schultz-*
> *McCarthy*

"Once upon a time, it was said that home-run hitters drive Cadillacs. Now it's ace hitters knock around in Lamborghinis."

> *Bud Collins*

"All Luciano Pavarotti can do is sing. It's likely that all Saul Bellow can do is write and probably Julia Child can't do much besides cook. But they're all champs just the same."

Bud Collins, on criticism early in Pete Sampras's career that all he could do was serve

"The serve was invented so the net could play."
Bill Cosby

"My service was not a weapon. I put it in there to start a point, not to ace anybody off the court."
Chris Evert

"My game plan is boom, boom, and more boom."
Peter Fleming

"Serve. Serve. Serve. Forty aces. Win. Boring."
Goran Ivanisevic, describing his game

"It's just hitting."
Goran Ivanisevic, describing his powerful serve

"I hate the second serve. If you don't get the first one in, it's a mulligan."

Chi Chi Rodriguez

"If your opponent tells you to take two, your ball was in."

Barry Tarshis, Tennis *magazine*

SERVICE BREAK

"These guys would sooner drop their girlfriends, agents, or accountants than their serve."

Bud Collins, on the 1994 Wimbledon final between Goran Ivanisevic and Pete Sampras

SERVICE WITH A SMILE

"Yours too."

Waiter at a restaurant, after Martina Navratilova told him his service was excellent

"I left at halftime."

> *Andre Agassi, on seeing* Les
> Misérables *on Broadway*

"The one thing I've always known is that people had better walk out of the stadium feeling that there's no way they'd rather spend their money."

> *Andre Agassi, on tennis as*
> *entertainment*

"This guy might not be ready for the floor show at the Copa, but he's putting on a dazzling display."

> *Mary Carillo, on a player having a*
> *great match*

"I'd even take up tennis to meet her."

> *Richard Simmons, declaring his*
> *fascination with Barbra Streisand,*
> *who was fascinated with Andre*
> *Agassi*

SIDE CHANGES

"The question is like asking what you think about when you're having dinner. When you're having dinner, you're thinking about the food, where the silverware is. . . . It's the same when you change sides."

> *Jeff Borowiak, asked what he thinks about when changing sides*

"It would have been like the TV cameras catching Troy Aikman or Emmitt Smith, brows furrowed, doing a crossword puzzle during time-outs in the Super Bowl."

> *Mike Lupica, on Jim Courier reading a book between changeovers in a tournament*

SKATE SPORTS

"If guys can't take a hit, they should go play tennis."

> *Bryan Marchment, Edmonton Oilers defenseman, on hockey players who complain about low hits*

"People look at these skates and say, 'Hey, you're into Rollerblading.' I'm not. I just don't like to walk."

>*Martina Navratilova, on*
>*Rollerblading*

SLUMPS

"At the moment, my best surface is my bed."

>*Jim Courier, on a year-long slump*

"My goal for 1983 is to be the Comeback Player of the Year."

>*Peter Fleming, on his 1982 slump*

"These days I can lose to any bozo at some club or park."

>*Vitas Gerulaitis*

"It's going to take time to get it back. But I've plenty of time to practice, seeing as I seem to be working only one day a week recently."

>*Ivan Lendl*

"When I got that far, I started believing I could beat anybody. It gave me a belief in myself that I certainly haven't lived up to since."

> *Chris Lewis, on a disappointing 1984 after making the 1983 Wimbledon final*

"If this year was a fish, I'd throw it back in."

> *Martina Navratilova, on a poor '88 season*

"You know how a normal worker feels on a Monday? Well, lately I've been having Mondays in the middle of the week."

> *Mats Wilander*

SMOKE—OUT

"I smoked 17 cigarettes . . . with one match. I'm going to ask Virginia Slims for an endorsement contract."

> *John Bassett, after watching his daughter Carling almost beat Chris Evert*

"I would like to thank the sponsor, even though I think it is a disgrace to smoke cigarettes."
> *Pat Cash, after winning an event*
> *sponsored by a cigarette company*

HAROLD SOLOMON

"He induces a kind of parabolic hypnosis and is a danger to low-flying sparrows."
> *Rex Bellamy, on Solomon's penchant*
> *for hitting a lot of high volleys*

"When you played Harold, you'd better bring your lunch and dinner—you might be out there all day."
> *Erik Van Dillon*

SOVIET SYSTEM

"He didn't do anything. They gave him a salary.
He has an office and sits in a small chair, big
stomach, lots of food. I cannot explain it to you."
*Andrei Medvedev, on his father's job
as an engineer during Communist
rule*

"It's a three-set match, and we're in the first set."
*Natalia Zvereva, on negotiating with
the Soviets to keep her winnings*

SPEED DEMON

"She plays like she's double-parked."
*Mary Carillo, on Andrea Jaeger's
inpatient style of play*

"I knew he was fast, but I never knew how fast
until I saw him playing tennis by himself."
Lou Holtz, on Rocket Ismail

"It doesn't affect me. I can play five points in 25 seconds."

> *Goran Ivanisevic, on a rule change*
> *allowing 20 instead of 25 seconds*
> *between points*

STEEL CITY

"You can have a good time anywhere. I've proven that in some of the worst dumps you can imagine. I once had a terrific summer in Pittsburgh."

> *Vitas Gerulaitis*

TALKIN' BASEBALL

"If this had been her kid brother, Randy Moffitt, a pitcher with the Toronto Blue Jays, she would have been yanked in the first inning."

> *Bud Collins, on Billie Jean King*
> *being demolished in the 1983*
> *Wimbledon semifinals*

"In baseball you have to leave your sensitivity at the door. If you can't take it, play tennis."

> *Ron Darling, on the sensitive nature of Gregg Jefferies*

"That's a lot of matches."

> *Stefan Edberg, on Cal Ripken breaking Lou Gehrig's consecutive-game record*

"He's one of the few guys in this town I can beat at tennis. I'm not going to let him go."

> *Clark Griffith, Minnesota Twins owner, on rumors that he was going to trade Rod Carew*

"It looked like a lot of Bettina Bunge backhands rolling in the outfield."

> *Mike Krukow, Giants pitcher, on the Giants giving up a lot of hits in an inning*

"Tennis players want quiet on the set. They throw the ball to themselves and hit it and can't have any noise. We've got 50,000 people screaming, doing the wave, and facing a 100-mph fastball. There's no comparison."

Davey Lopes, comparing baseball to tennis

"You want to know why I stopped coaching baseball and started coaching tennis? I had the A.L.'s Cy Young Award winner and I played him at third base."

Bill Lorenz, high-school coach of pitching great Jack Morris

"They acted like Yankee fans."

Martina Navratilova, on rowdy fans at the U.S. Open

"People used to ask Budge about his backhand and he'd tell everyone he copied Ted Williams's batting style."

Bill Talbert

"My only weaknesses are that I'm old, fat, and inexperienced."

> *Ted Williams, on learning to play tennis in his 70s*

ROSCOE TANNER

"The Great White Hummer."
> *Bud Collins*

TELEVISION

"As my uncle Studley says, 'This is as thrilling as marrying a woman after you've lived with her for a couple of years.'"

> *Bud Collins, on showing tennis matches on tape delay*

"I understand. I watch your television. I see that most of the shows are geared to a certain mentality. Would you want me to judge your culture by its television?"

Wojtek Fibak, Polish tennis star, asked how he felt about the popularity of Polish jokes in the United States

"My girlfriend told me over the phone that it's killing her staying up all night. The live TV gets to Australia at three in the morning."

Rod Frawley, on making the '81 semifinals at Wimbledon

"At least when you screw up on TV, you get another chance to do it over."

Martina Navratilova, who appeared on the TV show Hart to Hart, *comparing television to tennis*

"I went through that 10 years before he was even born."

> *Jimmy Connors, on John McEnroe's temper*

"I'm even too fast for you at that."

> *Pancho Gonzales, after Ted Schroder threw a tennis racket at him in disgust*

"I still break rackets, but now I do it in a positive way."

> *Goran Ivanisevic, on his new attitude*

"I'm a professor in the school of how to break the racket."

> *Goran Ivanisevic*

"It was interesting playing tennis with Mike—at least as long as his racket lasted."

> *Tom Landry, on playing tennis with Mike Ditka*

"You smiling jerk. I dare you to a fight."

John McEnroe, to a cameraman at the French Open who got too close to him

"I have temper. Who is perfect? If I cannot do the things on the court, I cannot play, I just get ulcers."

Ilie Nastase

"If I don't get mad sometimes, I can't play. It's like sitting at a table and watching the other guy eating. I don't enjoy it."

Ilie Nastase

"Bad behavior in tennis is like the extravagant second honeymoon you've always promised your wife; it's a source of constant conversation and debate, but nothing ever seems to get done about it."

Mark Preston, Tennis *magazine*

"It's me, and I'm like this. I'm going to throw my racket until I stop. It's quite normal. . . . It's been 13 or 15 years, so I got used to it."

Marc Rosset, on throwing rackets

"Actually, the person who stands out the most in my mind for jerky behavior is me."

    Pam Shriver

"If guys do it, it's macho, and if women do it, it's not very nice."

    Wendy Turnbull, on bad conduct

"Before anybody asked me what happened in the match, I want to say that everything that went on out there was really my fault."

    Tim Wilkinson, on refusing to shake hands with opponent Phil Dent after a match

TENNIS WISDOM

"A sport in which even an unseeded player can flower."

    Anonymous

"I hope that everyone at the end of their playing career, at whatever level, can say one thing I can say: 'It was fun.' That's what means the most."

    Arthur Ashe

"The very act of just hitting an oncoming, moving target while you're moving is all the challenge you'll need in your life."

Vic Braden

"If you can walk to the drinking fountain without falling over, you have the physical ability to play tennis well."

Vic Braden

"This game is going to humble you all your life. You start out playing a wall. What's the first thing you learn? You can't beat a wall."

Vic Braden

"I don't believe in doing what comes naturally. Usually, when you let it all hang out, what hangs out is pretty lousy."

Vic Braden

"Tennis is a game, not a jail sentence."

Vic Braden

"Everybody says be natural. . . . Nearly everything I've seen about tennis that's natural is wrong."

Vic Braden

"You don't play people. You play a ball."
Vic Braden

"Regardless of what John McEnroe once told an umpire—the *F* word in tennis is still fun."
Bud Collins

"Two people hitting a little ball over a net, and if you can't have some fun with it, then I think we're in trouble."
Bud Collins

"The minute you think you know all there is to know about tennis is the minute you start going down the tubes."
Jimmy Connors

"Unlike other sports, in tennis if you are getting killed, you are expected to stay out there and continue to get killed."
Bill Cosby

"Chances are, you are a much better player than you think you are. Then again, maybe not."
W. Timothy Gallwey, author

"Tennis to me is just like a chess game. You have to maneuver, you have to know your opponent's strengths and weaknesses."

Althea Gibson

"Good shot, bad luck, and hell are the five basic words to be used in a game of tennis, though these, of course, can be slightly amplified."

Virginia Graham

"It is not how you hold your racket, it's how you hold your mind."

Perry Jones, former U.S. Davis Cup coach

"Tennis and golf are best played, not watched."

Roger Kahn

"I love that the ball doesn't come over the net twice the same way in a lifetime, and that I'm always in the process of finding new shots."

Billie Jean King

"A perfect combination of violent action taking place in an atmosphere of total tranquillity."

Billie Jean King

"A game where you give other people a chance to lose to you."

Jack Kramer

"I made a decision about how I wanted to play the game. I would rather lose hitting the ball hard than win holding back."

Rod Laver

"I don't think I have any. I just throw dignity to the wind and think of nothing but the game."

Suzanne Lenglen, on her style

"If you see a tennis player who looks as if he is working very hard, then that means he can't be very good."

Helen Wills Moody

"In other sports, you can have a bad round or a bad inning or a bad game and still come back the next day. Tennis, you have a bad day, you go home."

Jim Murray

"Tennis is like football. You must set up the plays. If you set it up right, all you have to do is execute."

Martina Navratilova

"In my book a tennis player is the complete athlete. He has to have the speed of a sprinter, the endurance of a marathon runner, the agility of a boxer or fencer, and the gray matter of a good football quarterback."

Bobby Riggs

"Never make a move until you have six planned in advance."

Bill Riordan

"I think the players at the top in tennis, whether they're pros or club champions, recognize the strengths and weaknesses of their games, and then milk the strengths for all they're worth."

Pam Shriver

"I didn't waste shots. Every ball I hit had a purpose."

Bill Talbert

"Four out of five points are won on your opponent's errors. So just hit the ball back over the net."
Bill Talbert

"Big-time tennis will go on in spite of itself."
Bill Tilden

"Tennis matches are won by the man who hits the ball to the right place at the right time most often."
Bill Tilden

"My advice to young players is to see as much good tennis as possible and then attempt to copy the outstanding strokes of the former stars."
Bill Tilden

"Never change a winning game. Always change a losing one."
Bill Tilden

"Tennis is a very human game facing a great danger that it will be strangulated in a cat's cradle of unnecessary or inhumane rules."
Ted Tinling

"A tennis player is like a Swiss watch. There are 250 little wheels inside, and if one is not working properly, you have a problem."

Ion Tiriac

"When you make a great shot, when you've done it right, it's like dancing."

Edward Villella

"In tennis, if something is working well, it is usually best to stick with it."

Ellsworth Vines

THAT'S THE WAY THE BALL BOUNCES

"As long as they don't put in speed bumps, I have no complaints."

Martina Navratilova, on a couple of bad bounces

"My love for the game and combat counteracts my age."

Jimmy Connors, at age 36

"When you pack your suitcase, you're not going out to play tournaments. You're going to war."

Steve Krulevitz, touring pro

"Wouldn't you want me in the front lines?"

*Martina Navratilova, on the
controversy over gays in the military*

"We're going to send Spiro in there with a golf club and a tennis racket."

*Richard Nixon, suggesting that
Vice President Agnew, who had hit
bystanders on a golf course and a
tennis court with balls, go to
Cambodia as a peace negotiator*

"Strokes are the weapons with which you fight your tennis battles. The better the weapon, the greater the chance of victory."

Bill Tilden

TIEBREAKERS

"It's like rolling dice."

> *John Newcombe, on the innovation of*
> *the tiebreaker*

BILL TILDEN

"When Tilden was at his best, he was more of an artist than nine-tenths of the artists I know."

> *Franklin Adams*

"It is the beauty of the game that Tilden loves; it's the chase always, rather than the quarry."

> *Franklin Adams*

"I never got close to Tilden. I didn't particularly like him, and I'm sure he returned the favor."

> *Allison Danzig*

"I can't beat him. I can't beat the son of a bitch. I can't beat him."

> *Bill Johnston, on his rivalry*
> *with Tilden*

"He seems to experience a strong fascination over his opponents as well as his spectators. Tilden, even when beaten, leaves the impression on the public mind that he was superior to the victor."

> *René Lacoste*

"It took all of us to contain the great Tilden, not just any one of us."

> *René Lacoste, on the famous French*
> *Musketeers*

"Tilden is the only player in the world. The rest of us are second-graders."

> *Gerald Patterson*

"Hell, Bill, you intimidate him—just like you do all the rest of us."

> *Wayne Sabin, after Tilden asked*
> *Sabin how he always beat Bobby*
> *Riggs*

ION TIRIAC

"You always feel you should walk right through Tiriac, but he's much tougher to beat than you think."

> *John Newcombe, on Tiriac's inner*
> *toughness*

TOOTH DECAY

"I feel better as John McEnroe now. Maybe losing a little wisdom helps."

> *John McEnroe, on having his wisdom*
> *teeth removed*

TRAVEL PLANS

"It's a Greek tragedy. I'm getting the work I want and I'm inflicting pain on myself by being away so much."

> *Mary Carillo, on how her travel*
> *schedule as an announcer affects*
> *her marriage*

"His travel schedule was so hectic, he must have Patty Hearst's agent."

> *Bud Collins, on John Newcombe's*
> *hectic traveling pace*

WENDY TURNBULL

"Wendy is not that good technically, but they don't call her the Rabbit for nothing."

> *Virginia Wade, after she lost to*
> *Turnbull in the U.S. Open*

U.S. OPEN

"The Stadium Court looks as though it had been hurled together by an unusually corrupt city official and his 20 or 30 cousins in the construction business."

> *Martin Amis, British author, on the*
> *Stadium Court at the U.S. Tennis*
> *Center in Flushing Meadows,*
> *New York*

"This is the most difficult to win. You have the crowd here, you have the heat here, you have the noise here."

> *Boris Becker, comparing the*
> *U.S. Open to the other Grand*
> *Slam tournaments*

"There's a different breed of cats coming out here. Instead of hoi polloi, we're now getting Johnny Six-Pack."

> *Mike Blanchard, on fan behavior at*
> *the '77 U.S. Open*

"Winning at Wimbledon was wonderful and it meant a lot to me. But there is nothing like winning the championship of your own country."

> *Don Budge*

"He lost his lunch, but not his title."

> *Bud Collins, on Pete Sampras*
> *throwing up during his five-set*
> *victory over Alex Corretja in the*
> *'96 quarterfinals*

"The worst pounding of a Frenchman by an American since champ Jack Dempsey flattened Georges Carpentier."

> *Bud Collins, on Pete Sampras demolishing Cedric Pioline in the '93 finals*

"The U.S. Open is the only place in America where you can't trade in your Mercedes-Benz for a hamburger."

> *Bud Collins*

"New Yorkers want blood."

> *Jimmy Connors, on the loud, vociferous crowds at Flushing Meadows*

"I like any title with the letters 'U.S.' in front of it. To me, the U.S. Open is the most important tournament in the world."

> *Jimmy Connors*

"New Yorkers love it when you spill your guts out there. You spill your guts at Wimbledon, they make you stop and clean it up."

> *Jimmy Connors*

"I gave them my guts, and my blood, and my flesh and my skin. I couldn't give anymore."

> *Jimmy Connors, on losing the*
> *'84 U.S. Open in five sets to*
> *John McEnroe*

"Playing inside a toilet bowl."

> *Jim Courier, on the Stadium Court*
> *at the U.S. Tennis Center*

"I hate coming to New York. I hate the city, I hate the tournament, and I hate Flushing Meadows. They could drop an A-bomb on this place."

> *Kevin Curren*

"If a Hollywood movie studio called in the summer and offered me an Academy Award role in a picture, they'd have to wait to do the shooting till after the Open. And I always leave the following Monday open in case it rains."

> *Alan King, on his love of the*
> *U.S. Open*

"A bloody cow pasture most of the time."

> *Rod Laver, on the lawn at Forest*
> *Hills, the former site of the U.S.*
> *Open*

"Sort of a high-class call girl for corporate New York."

> Mike Lupica, on how major
> corporations have taken over the
> U.S. Open

"Wimbledon is special, peaceful. Here is like a zoo."

> Hana Mandlikova

"It's just the worst atmosphere I've met. Seriously, you have only one place you can be in—the players' lounge—and it is so crowded and it is so loud that you cannot be there more than one hour to be normal, to be calm."

> Andrei Medvedev

"It's been so long since an American woman won that the orchestra is going to have to send out for the sheet music to the 'Star-Spangled Banner.'"

> Jim Murray, on the 15-year drought
> of American-born women winning the
> U.S. Open

"Wimbledon is the red-carpet showcase of tennis. The U.S. Open is a ****ing zoo."

> John Newcombe

"Going to the Open for him was like going to a beer garden, and he doesn't drink that well."
Tony Pickard, coach of Stefan Edberg

"At the U.S. Open, it's not just a sport, it's an adventure."
Michael Stich

"It is like a hungry man who never eats. Then he has a piece of bread. Then a sandwich. Then a steak. Then he wants to go to the palace."
Guillermo Vilas, on winning the 1977 U.S. Open

"Wimbledon is perfect to play tennis in, while Flushing Meadows is just the opposite, like playing in an airport."
Mats Wilander

VACATION

"I am perfectly happy on a vacation if there is some sand and water and a tennis court."
David Dinkins

GUILLERMO VILAS

"Tennis in Argentina can be divided into before Vilas and after Vilas—not only in international competition but at every level."

Miguel Gorrissen, tennis promoter

ELLSWORTH VINES

"When they taught Elly how to keep score, they taught him everything he needed to know."

Wilmer Allison, on Vines's great natural ability

"Elly Vines never saw anything particularly difficult about hitting, catching, throwing, or putting a ball. It came as natural to him as crooning to Crosby or dealing cards to Nick the Greek."

Jim Murray, on Vines being an all-sports star

VITAS

"I do a lot of sleeping. I go, thinking I'll exercise, but I usually end up in a corner watching the other guys pump iron. I love to watch."

Vitas Gerulaitis, on his exercise routine

"Nobody beat Vitas Gerulaitis 17 times in a row."

Vitas Gerulaitis, on beating Jimmy Connors after 16 straight losses

"He has had more dance cards than scorecards in the last year."

Lesley Visser, on Gerulaitis's 1981 season until the U.S. Open

WE ARE FAMILY

"I named her Zina because I wanted a Z word. . . . She was the seventh—and that was definitely going to be the last."

Zina Garrison's mother

"I've been sleeping with his mother."

Dick Leach, USC tennis coach,
on how he recruited his star
tennis-playing son Mike to play
for USC

"I don't think of it as losing to my brother. I think of it as losing to the second-ranked player in the tournament."

Sandy Mayer, on losing to his
brother Gene

"Every emotion you can imagine was there—from worrying about how he's doing to worrying that he might beat me."

John McEnroe, on playing brother
Patrick in the finals of a 1992
tournament

"It's just like you all expected—Edberg, Lendl, McEnroe, and Becker."

Patrick McEnroe, on making it to the
Australian Open semifinals

"I beat their mother when I was a girl at a tournament in Bulgaria. Obviously, I didn't beat her badly. She managed to have three daughters after that."

> *Martina Navratilova, on beating*
> *Yulia Maleeva, mother of tennis pros*
> *Magdalena, Katerina, and Manuela*

"I'd like to see the pigeons they get to play on that one."

> *Pam Shriver, on rumors that Peter*
> *Graf was starting his own tennis*
> *association*

WEATHER WATCH

"If a rainy day comes, I don't have an umbrella."

> *Vitas Gerulaitis, on spending*
> *everything he makes*

"When a guy named Noah talks about rain, you listen."

> *Yannick Noah fan, after overhearing*
> *Noah tell someone it wasn't going to*
> *rain during a tournament*

WEDDED BLISS

"This is the first time I've ever seen Borg on his knees."

> *Ilie Nastase, on Bjorn Borg kneeling at the altar when he married Mariana Simionescu*

WEIGHTY ISSUES

"It's simple. I can't remember the last time I played a full uninterrupted set of tennis. It's crazy, I know, but I'm just too busy trying to get everybody else to play."

> *Vic Braden, on being out of shape*

"You're a fat football player, a fat baseball player, even a fat basketball player, a fat prizefighter, a fat golfer, lots of fat golfers, but never a fat tennis player."

> *Jim Murray*

"He's so flat, he could fax himself to a tournament."

Jim Murray, on Michael Stich

WHAT'S THE MATTER WITH KIDS TODAY?

"These two little kids came up to me and they said, 'We don't want your autograph. We want Tracy's. Can you forge it?'"

John Austin, Tracy's brother

"It is a stupid idea. The kids are always screaming and make stupid remarks."

Marc Rosset, on Children's Day at the French Open

WHITE CHRISTMAS

"A 60-foot yacht and a topspin backhand lob."

Bob Lutz, reciting his Christmas list

"A forehand volley and Cheryl Ladd."

> *Eliot Teltscher, reciting his*
> *Christmas list*

MATS WILANDER

"Agassi's forehand is not the biggest weapon in tennis today. Mats Wilander's brain is."

> *Jay Berger*

"You fed my family and paid my mortgage last year."

> *Mike Leach, to Wilander, whom he*
> *upset at the '85 Lipton tournament*

"I really enjoy that Lendl went out, because now I'm the best one left in the tournament from Greenwich, Connecticut."

> *Mats Wilander, after Ivan Lendl was*
> *upset in the French Open*

"The easiest way to become a member here is to win the championship."

> *Anonymous, on the All-England*
> *Tennis Club*

"If God had meant Wimbledon to be played in great weather, he would have put it in Acapulco."

> *Anonymous*

"If I eat another strawberry, I'm going to throw up."

> *Tracy Austin, after making it to*
> *the third round at age 14*

"This is where I was born in 1985."

> *Boris Becker, said in 1992 about*
> *Centre Court*

"Faulty celestial plumbing was an accepted feature, like strawberries and cream."

> *Bud Collins, on rain at Wimbledon*

"Playing as though she were a deadline-dreading Cinderella in glass sneakers, Martina turned her victims into pumpkins."

> *Bud Collins, on Martina Navratilova's dominance of Wimbledon in 1981, when her matches averaged less than an hour*

"Wimbledon without Borg seems like the Vatican without the pope."

> *Bud Collins*

"Bout between the American Mr. Growl and the Czech Mr. Scowl."

> *Bud Collins, on the '83 Wimbledon semifinals between John McEnroe and Ivan Lendl*

"There is now."

> *Bud Collins, asked, after Malivai Washington made it to the '96 Wimbledon finals, if there was a saint named Malivai*

"They sell everything but the toilet seats, but you just don't see it."

Donald Dell, on how Wimbledon makes millions of dollars

"Exude rectitude in all directions."

J. P. Donleavy, Wimbledon official, characterizing Wimbledon

"I'm a pretty horrendous grass-court player, but I guess I'm pumping up the game a little now."

Pat Dupre, on making it to the Wimbledon semifinals

"It's always the same. Either it's rainy with sunny intervals or sunny with rainy intervals."

Pat Dupre, on the weather at Wimbledon

"An occasion that consumes a country."

Chris Evert

"This is where my heart is, no matter where in the world I am. I know and love every inch of that court. It's my place."

Billie Jean King, on Centre Court

"I love the Centre Court. I wish I could hug it sometimes."

Billie Jean King

"I don't like it, but I will play there. It will be wet, and I will take some books with me to read. But I will play."

Ivan Lendl

"At Wimbledon, I have spent more time under water than the *Andrea Doria*."

Mike Lupica

"I was thinking, 'Oh my God, what am I going to do?' I have to make a curtsy there and a curtsy there. I was thinking, "What if I don't do well?"

Conchita Martinez, after winning Wimbledon in 1994

"If you say anything during a tennis match, they make it seem like you committed murder or something."

John McEnroe

"Apart from bloody Wimbledon, I've won every major tournament. So the hell with Wimbledon. For me, life is just beginning to be fun."

Ilie Nastase, on his retirement

"Finally, I won the SOB tournament and I take my trophy and go all around the stadium, bowing to the people and giving the finger to everybody."

Ilie Nastase, recounting a dream he had

"I prefer to consider my love for Wimbledon a rational reverence."

Martina Navratilova, asked if she was obsessed with Wimbledon

"Just about every day I think about tennis, and tennis is Wimbledon."

Martina Navratilova, on her love of Wimbledon

"You can find out anything you want to know about a person by putting him on the Centre Court. It has a lot to do with your breaking point."

John Newcombe

"There's an electricity out there which lets you go through games and sets and you don't realize what's happening."

John Newcombe

"Breakfast at Wimbledon turned out to be Continental."

Ed Pope, columnist, after John McEnroe defeated Jimmy Connors in three easy sets in 1984

"I tried to get an indoor facility built near here, but it was voted down solidly. They voted against tennis in Wimbledon."

Roger Taylor

"There's no sense of tomorrow in Wimbledon. They're drowning in yesterday."

Ted Tinling

"Wimbledon is an enclave of old England, anachronistic in the nicest way."

Ted Tinling

"It rains 90 percent of the time, and there are no practice courts unless you're one of the top ten."

Butch Walts, on why he doesn't like Wimbledon

"I felt pretty confident that the match was in my hands when I hit the final ace and we were about to shake hands. I knew at that point I had him."

Mal Washington, asked when he felt confident of victory facing Thomas Enquist in the third round of the '96 Wimbledon

"You sit around and wait. That's tennis anyway. It's sometimes good, sometimes bad, mostly bad, I'd say."

Mats Wilander, on rain delays at Wimbledon

"Of all the evocative names in sports . . . I do not believe that any has more significance or rings the bells of memory more loudly and clearly than Wimbledon."

Herbert Warren Wind

WIMPS

"I consider anyone who tanks a wimp."
Brad Gilbert

"If muscles are all that matter, how come John McEnroe is No. 1 in the world? He's a wimp."
Martina Navratilova

WINNING

"When you're on a roll, you stay on it, until something happens."
Jimmy Arias

"You win alone, just as you lose alone."
Arthur Ashe

"It may sound dull, but you'll never get bored with winning. I've never heard anyone complain, 'Nuts, I won again.'"
Vic Braden

"Outwardly, I appreciate calm, but inside I was boiling. To be the best, you have to care mightily."
Don Budge

"My ambition is to play perfect tennis. Then I will always win."
Maureen Connolly

"If you're going to play tennis, then I say play it the best you can. That's just the way I am. If it wasn't tennis, I'd be number one at whatever I was doing. That's something born in me."
Jimmy Connors

"I think about what the other player's face would look like at the net if they beat me."
Chris Evert, on what motivates her to win

"When I was in junior tennis, they called me a punk. Now I'm colorful. You know what the difference is—colorful guys win."
Vitas Gerulaitis

"You know we are all capable of great shotmaking. So what puts me ahead of the rest? Better physical conditioning and wanting to win more."

Ivan Lendl

"Tennis is a different game. There's nobody out there who has perfect stuff. The idea is to win with what you've got."

John McEnroe

"When you get ahead, keep your opponent down, stand on him, kick him, and don't let up."

Gardnar Mulloy, on winning

"I try to make it as boring as I can."

Martina Navratilova, on winning easily

"Lots of people in tennis strive to be a Goliath with the attitude of a David."

Barbara Potter

"For me, for my career, it's not the money. It's not the commercials. It's the titles."

Pete Sampras

WOMEN

"If someone says it's not feminine, I say screw it."
>*Rosie Casals, responding to assertions that tennis is not a feminine sport*

"You know the ball is going to come back twenty million times before you get a point."
>*Rosie Casals, on the state of women's tennis in the 1980s*

WORLD TEAM TENNIS

"Investors who believed in faster ways of burning money than using it in a wood stove kept WTT afloat."
>*Bud Collins*

"WTT is the most unprofessional, kinky, bizarre, and ridiculous sports gambit to come along since Tony Galento."
>*Curry Kirkpatrick*

"The sport's Coney Island."
>	*Mike Lupica*

"I kept hearing the Braves were trying to bring Atlanta its first-ever pro sports championship. I guess some people have short memories."
>	*Martina Navratilova, on the Atlanta*
>	*Thunder, which won the WTT*
>	*championship*

"At least no one got pregnant."
>	*Ion Tiriac, looking at the bright side*
>	*of the first year of WTT*

WORLD TOUR

"They drive too fast, they charge too much, and they don't speak English."
>	*Bud Collins, on why foreign*
>	*cabdrivers are similar to American*
>	*cabdrivers*

"It's not my head I've been hitting. . . . It's my Adam's apple."

Chip Hooper, 6'6" tennis pro, on hotels in Japan

"It looks like London to me, only drearier. I hope the people are nicer."

John McEnroe, on Dublin

"I'd go sight-seeing, but I don't think there's much to see in this place."

John McEnroe, on London

"It would be a nice place if you took all the people out of the city."

John McEnroe, on Paris

"It's a very clean city. Everybody drinks beer and Pepsi and has a good time."

Ilie Nastase, on Bucharest

"I have to feel good in a city to play well in it. I've just never discovered what makes London tick."

Yannick Noah, on never playing well at Wimbledon

"You figure there's eight trillion people in China, and she was No. 1 there—it says something."

Pam Shriver, after barely beating
Hu Na

"Everybody in England is a show-off. I'm just one who'll admit it."

Ted Tinling

"Tennis players love jewelry, because it's one of the few things worth owning that you can take around the world with you."

Ted Tinling

INDEX

236